MIS-MATCHED TO MISS MATCHED

MIS-MATCHED TO MISS MATCHED

SUZANNE PUREWAL

Purewal Publishing, LLC
Noblesville, Indiana

Published by
Purewal Publishing, LLC
176 W. Logan Street #105
Noblesville, Indiana 46060-1437
www.SuzannePurewal.com

All rights reserved. No part of this publication may be reproduced, stored in a retrieval system or transmitted, in any form, or by any means, electronic, mechanical, recorded, photocopied, or otherwise, without the prior written permission of both the copyright owner and the above publisher of this book, except by a reviewer who may quote brief passages in a review.

The scanning, uploading, and distribution of this book via the Internet or via any other means without the permission of the publisher is illegal and punishable by law. Please purchase only authorized electronic editions and do not participate in or encourage electronic piracy or copyrightable materials. Your support of the author's rights is appreciated.

All rights reserved.

Copyright © 2017 by Suzanne Purewal

Cover Art and Design by Joseph S. Anderson – TheForgottenArtist.com

Author Photograph by Hether Miles – hethermilesphotography.com

ISBN: 978-0-9829048-4-8 (print version)

ISBN: 978-0-9829048-5-5 (e-book version)

Library of Congress Card Catalog Number: 2017938513

Printed in the United States of America

If you purchased this book without a cover, you should be aware that this book is stolen property. It was reported as "unsold and destroyed" to the publisher, and neither the author nor the publisher has received any payment for this "stripped book."

To My Muse, Lynn
For your unwavering support, fierce determination,
and eternal optimism

Contents

Preface	xi
Disclaimer	xiv
Additional Titles by Suzanne Purewal	xv
Mom's Thoughts on Online Dating	1
Mom's Thoughts on Online Dating, Part II	4
Mis-Matched	6
The Lewd, The Crude, and The Ugly	10
Worst Pickup Lines Ever	15
Searching For Mrs. Robinson	19
The Old Bait and Switch	25
Doctors & Chemists & A Cowboy, Oh My!	32
I'm Not Like Other Guys	38
A Motherly Type of Love	43
The Foreign Contingent	45
A Handful of Mixed Nuts	50
It Finally Happened!	56

Fright or Delight?	61
The Twelve Days of Christmas	63
Just Say, "No!"	67
Could Business Lead to Pleasure?	72
Dysfunctional Dates Abound	75
My Big, Fat Greek Tragedy	81
Awkward Moments	84
It's Hard to Be Arm Candy	87
When Will I Be Loved?	90
A Shape-Shifter, A Sex Addict, and A Dominant Male	95
Drunk and Drunker	102
Not So Helpful Dating Advice	109
You Want Me To Do What?	112
The Time I Completely Lost My Mind	118
Over the River and Through the Woods	121
The Sound of Silence	124
Not So Elite	127
Déjà Vu	132
My Twelve Days of Christmas	134
When Push Came to Shove	138
Jumping Off The Crazy Train	142
Expect the Unexpected	144

Epilogue	*149*
About The Author	*151*

Preface

As I recited my wedding vows to my betrothed in 1993, I intended to remain married until death parted us. Apparently, He-Who-Shall-Not-Be-Named made different plans. On January 1, 2011, I was blindsided and devastated when he informed me that he was divorcing me. I had no idea what would come next. However, I knew I would survive.

I survived cancer and being downsized from my job. I would live through my husband walking out on me too. Hey, just throw in a pickup truck and a dog, and my life is a country song.

Well, except I can't have a dog or any pet for that matter. I am severely allergic to all animals, anaphylactic, throat-closes-up, death-is-imminent allergic.

At this juncture, I decided that either God had a warped sense of humor or someone had cast the *malocchio* on me. For non-Italian readers, the *malocchio* is the evil eye.

Fortunately, I passed the *malocchio* test. That left the option that God was testing me. For what? I don't know. However, if history was any indication, it would require perseverance and fortitude on my part.

The dating world has changed a great deal in the past two decades, and not for the better, mind you. I would not have believed some of these things myself, had I not lived through them.

This book chronicles my epic saga of online dating adventures, nay misadventures. Some of these stories were originally posted as articles on my blog, *Pursuing My Passion*. However, there are plenty of new chapters and expanded content.

All of the stories are true. As the saying goes, "Fact is stranger than fiction." I agree with that sentiment wholeheartedly. I have this entire book that proves that theory. In that spirit, to preserve the true essence of the men's characters and e-mail exchanges, I did not correct the grammar or punctuation errors.

My bizarre dating odyssey began after my divorce was finalized. Initially, I attempted to date friends of friends or acquaintances of friends. One guy wanted to buy me an engagement ring after our first date. Did I mention that his ex-wife lived in his basement? Then, there was a wealthy playboy. He just wanted to have sex with anyone, anywhere. Another man was married and wanted a mistress.

Other men were in transition. Some were divorced, others were not. All of those men were simply looking for hookups, no strings attached. The majority of them were much older than me.

Suffice it to say, those experiences jaded me. I wanted to find a man who moved me and set my soul on fire. I dreamt of a man who mirrored my hopeless romantic side. My wish was to find that one man who would not only hold my hand, but also my heart. I intended to search the ends of the earth, or at least the tri-state area, for that special man who I would love and adore for the rest of my life. And he would love me as much as I loved him. We would be happy and truly in love, supporting one another in all things, and making our hopes and dreams reality. We would take comfort knowing we would always be together, through the good times and the bad.

With those lofty hopes and dreams in mind, in March 2013, I signed up on one of the most popular online dating websites. Never in a million years did I ever think I would have to resort to online dating. But alas, I found that meeting a decent man any other way was virtually impossible. So, I bit the bullet. I opted for the six-month deal with the guarantee that if I didn't find anyone in that time period, I would get another six months free. That plan cost about $100. I figured it was a good investment, if I got a husband out of it.

After entering all of my pertinent information, I selected the criteria for my match. I chose all eye and hair colors, all body types, except obese, all ethnicities, and all religions. I decided on an age range five years on either side of my age.

Due to my allergies, I clearly stated that I was looking for a non-smoker and someone without any pets. Since my allergic reaction to animals is anaphylactic, having pets was a deal-breaker.

Then, I listed my interests, including playing the guitar, singing, writing, attending live musical and theatrical performances, hiking in National Parks, and road trips.

It took approximately an hour to complete the remaining sections of my profile. Then, I went "live" and began the adventure of a lifetime!

Disclaimer

The content in this book is based on the author's personal experiences and is meant for entertainment purposes only. The opinions expressed throughout this book are the opinions of the author.

The material contained within is not for the purpose of recommending any online dating service nor is it intended to provide advice on selecting an online dating service. All of the online dating services the author used were reputable, established businesses that have facilitated successful relationships among countless individuals. The author's experiences with these sites are her own and are in no way representative of any other individual's experiences.

Online dating services make no guarantees, either express or implied, regarding the ultimate compatibility with any person you meet through their services.

Additional Titles by Suzanne Purewal

Embracing Destiny
Challenging Destiny
From 14 to 41

Mom's Thoughts on Online Dating

The mere thought of me plunging into online dating sent my mother into a bit of a tizzy. But for those of us over forty, let's face it, we do not have many other alternatives.

I love Mom dearly for her advice and for wanting the very best for me. Sometimes, I find humor in our daily exchanges. Yes, I talk to my mother (and father) every day. Despite the miles that physically separate us, we are a close-knit family. I would not want it any other way. (The close-knit part, not the distance part!)

This was the first conversation we had about online dating.

Mom stated, "I don't like the idea of you doing this online dating thing."

I sighed heavily. "Uh huh."

Seriously, she inquired, "Did you see *Criminal Minds* this week?"

"Yes."

"You saw what happened to those girls?"

"Yes."

"I'd feel better if one of your friends set you up with someone."

"You know they tried. But the guys were all *old*."

"Age shouldn't matter."

"In theory, I agree. But I'm not attracted to old men."

"They all weren't *that* old."

"They were closer to your age than to mine. That doesn't work for me."

Mom pressed, "How will you know if these online men are who they say they are?"

"I don't. But that could happen no matter how I meet a guy."

She advised, "Don't ever meet a man at his house."

"I know. I'm not stupid. I would meet him at a restaurant or some public place."

"One with good lighting in the parking lot."

Rolling my eyes, I replied, "Yes, one with good lighting."

"So how does this work exactly?"

I explained, "Everyone fills out a profile with interests and stuff. Then some computer program matches us up based on our profiles."

"But they could lie and use someone else's picture."

"Yes, they could. But that would be pretty stupid. And I wouldn't sign up for a free site. I'd use one you have to pay for. That should weed out some of the riff-raff."

"I love you, and I just want you to be happy."

"I know. I love you too."

"Let's change the subject."

I breathed a sigh of relief. "Okay. Thank you."

"So, did you see the segment on the news about The Villages?"

(The Villages is a popular retirement community in Florida.)

"No, I didn't."

"Well, there has been a drastic rise in STDs among the residents. Since the women can't get pregnant, they're not practicing safe sex. The men are spreading venereal diseases around like wildfire."

And that's my mom—master of subtlety!

Note: The STD issue in retirement communities has been a hot topic of conversation over the years. Craig Pittman, author of, *Oh, Florida!: How America's Weirdest State Influences the Rest of the Country*, highlighted the issue in an online article, dated July 22, 2013. The topic is also referenced in an article, dated June 4, 2014, on the Villages-News.com website.

Mom's Thoughts on Online Dating, Part II

After Mom read my blog post on our conversation, she asked me to clarify her position on a certain subject. And being the good Catholic daughter I am, I obliged.

Mom said, "I liked your post. It was funny. But I didn't like how you ended it. I don't want people to think that I condone sex outside of marriage. Because I don't."

I replied, "I know you don't."

"But all of the other people reading your blog don't know that. Nobody should be having sex, unless they're married."

"I know."

She quickly added, "To each other."

I laughed.

"Period."

Still laughing, I acknowledged, "I know."

She continued, "It's not right. Fix it."

"Okay, Mom. I'll write another post."

Satisfied her point had been made, she responded, "Good. Thank you."

"It's the least I can do. I wouldn't want you to lose any sleep over it."

"I have other things to lose sleep over. And you should put something in your online profile too. That way those men won't get the wrong idea."

I sighed heavily as I rolled my eyes. "Mom, I can weed out those guys without a grand declaration in writing."

She warned me, "Some men are animals and just want sex."

"I know. A lot has changed in the last twenty years. But that part has remained the same. I dealt with them before, I can deal with them again."

In her concerned motherly tone, she said, "I just worry about you."

Appreciative, I answered, "I know. Thank you. Don't worry."

"Of course I'll worry. And I'll say a Rosary."

"You and me both, Mom! You and me both!"

Mis-Matched

Navigating the alien world of online dating is challenging and not for the faint of heart. I did not anticipate the barrage of likes, winks, favorites, and e-mails. Monitoring and managing my account was a full-time job for the first two weeks. Apparently, that's what happens with "fresh meat." Who knew?

Unfortunately, many of the "wanna be" suitors looked as if they lived in the back hills of Kentucky, in an underground bunker, with enough firepower to survive the apocalypse. I kept hearing banjo music in my head as I scanned the photos. Seriously.

My apologies to any readers who are gun owners, are from Kentucky, and/or are bluegrass music fans.

And don't get me started on the shirtless pictures. Or the bathroom pictures. Or the blurry pictures. Everyone who has a cell phone has a camera. All they had to do was hand their phones to a friend and have him/her take a decent picture. Then again, perhaps these guys don't have friends. That would explain a lot!

I did not respond to any of the likes, winks, or favorites. I decided if a guy was too lazy to send me an e-mail, he wasn't worth my time. I sorted through the e-mail candidates. They ranged in age from 24 to 79. They lived all over the country.

Here is a taste of what I experienced in my first week of e-mail exchanges.

Bachelor #1 was a 27-year-old sales representative living in Indianapolis.

He began, "Your eyes are beautiful. I would love to meet you."

"Thank you. I'm flattered. But I'm old enough to be your mother. You need to find someone your own age."

"I don't mind. You don't look old."

"But I am older. You're young and good-looking. I am sure you can find someone your own age. There are some great places around town that have live music and attract people your age."

"You are sweet and helpful. I really want to meet you."

"I'm sorry. No. I'm too old."

"I like that you're older. I could use a teacher."

"Definitely not. No. Look for someone your own age and have fun. I wish you luck finding a match."

Then this poor misguided young man sent me a frowning emoticon.

Bachelor #2 was a 49-year-old model living in Kentucky.

He typed, "I am impressed with your beauty and intelligence."

"Thank you. I see you are a professional model. What type of modeling do you do?"

"All types of modeling. Do you have a full-length picture you can send me?"

"I don't have any full-length pics. The ones I posted in my profile are recent."

"Your face is beautiful but I won't talk to anyone unless I see a full-length pic. I've been disappointed too many times."

"I am about 5'7" and weigh 130 pounds."

"Thanks for that but I need to see how you carry it."

I thought to myself, *This guy is a shallow jackass. Un-freaking-real.*

I replied, "Well, I'm sure I would pass your test. But I have surgical scars, and I'm sure you'll find those totally unacceptable. Good luck finding a match who meets your standards."

No response at all. No surprise there!

Bachelor #3 was a 48-year-old sales rep living in Indy.

He was eager. "Wow! I want to meet you."

"Thank you. But my profile clearly states that I am severely allergic to animals, and I won't date anyone who has an animal. You have two dogs."

"So we could be perfect soulmates but because I have dogs you won't meet me?"

"Right. Sorry. I wish you luck finding a match."

"Screw you. You look sickly anyway."

Yikes! I'm sensing abusive tendencies and anger management issues.

I finally found one that passed the e-mail test. Bachelor #4 gave me his full name and links to his business website and Facebook page. So, I looked him up.

He was a 45-year-old millionaire with an impressive resume. I agreed to meet him at Panera for coffee. However, I don't drink coffee. I ordered lemonade.

Remember that impressive resume? That was the extent of his ability to wow me. He talked on his cell phone the entire time he waited in line to order. Then, he texted the entire forty minutes of our "meet and greet." Well, it doesn't take a rocket scientist to figure out why he was divorced.

So, it was back to the website for me!

Bachelor #5 was a 47-year-old fireman living in Carmel.

In an effort to prove he read my profile, he wrote, "I see you love National Parks. We seem to have a lot in common."

I answered, "Sorry, but I'm allergic to animals. I wish you luck finding a match."

"Wow!!! I've never been called an animal before. So how can you say that if you haven't even met me yet?!?"

"Lol. Nice sense of humor. But you have a cat, and I'm allergic to animals."

"I knew what you meant. Just wanted to see if you'd type back. Best of luck to you."

"Thanks! The same to you!"

And that, my dear readers, was just the tip of the iceberg.

The Lewd, The Crude, and The Ugly

The next group of men were quite colorful and uncouth.

Bachelor #6 did not list his profession. This 43-year-old managed to pass the e-mail phase, so we decided to talk on the phone.

In a strong voice, he said, "I'd like to meet you in person."

"Okay. What day is good for you?"

"Well, I coach my son's baseball team. We have practices or games every day."

"I see."

He proposed, "You could come watch me coach the double-header this Saturday, and then I could come to your house, and you can make me dinner."

Are you kidding me?

Seeking confirmation, I asked, "You want me to watch you coach all day, and then make you dinner? Did I get that right?"

"Yeah. I'd make you dinner, but I'm living with a buddy until I get back on my feet."

"I'm sorry, but that doesn't work for me."

With indignation in his voice, he asked, "Just because I don't have my own place?"

"No. It's everything else."

"Whaddya mean?"

Wow! Where to begin?

I spelled it out for him. "I don't know you, so there's no way I'm telling you where I live, let alone cook you dinner. And spending an entire day sitting with strangers on hard bleachers watching you coach a bunch of 12-year-olds is not my idea of a date. Shall I go on?"

"You're high maintenance, aren't you?"

"Not even close. We're done here. Good luck finding a match."

"Whatever."

Bachelor #7 was in sales. His profile listed his age as 89 years old. His picture showed he was much younger. He was seeking women, ages 24-36.

He e-mailed me, "You have a fantastic smile. I want to get to know you."

"Thank you. I am definitely out of your "Seeking Women" age range. And I can not have children. So, if you need to have children, then I'm out. If you're still interested, let me know, and be kind enough to tell me your real age."

"I'm 46. Let's chat."

"Ok. On the phone or in person?"

"U look a little innocent."

That was an odd comment. Hmmm ...

Wondering where this conversation would lead, I said, "That innocent look is a result from twelve years of Catholic school."

He replied, "I may be too wild for your taste. I may corrupt u. I did read fifty shades."

Huh? I read it again. *Oh, good Lord!*

I responded quickly, "I read the first book in the *50 Shades* series. I am not into S&M or bondage. So, if you like it rough, you'll need to look elsewhere."

"Ok"

Whoa! Dodged a bullet there. Or at least handcuffs ...

Moving right along ... Bachelor #8 was a 35-year-old in advertising.

His opening line was unique. "I'm looking for a woman who can handle me. You look like you could."

"Not exactly sure what you mean by that. I'm not looking for a bad boy."

"I'm a good boy most of the time. Trust me. I need a woman who can handle me. I'm enormous and I can keep it going all night long."

Laughing as I typed, "With an ego that big, I'm surprised you haven't hurt yourself by now. It must be tough dragging that bravado around everywhere you go."

"Bitch"

Oh well, I've been called worse!

Bachelor #9 was 51 years old and worked in communications. Normally, I try not to judge a book by its cover. But this guy took the creepy, scary, stalker, troll look to a new level. He should have stayed under the bridge. God forgive me.

Quick and to the point, his e-mail stated, "You're pretty. I want to meet you."

I would not have met him in a million years. "I'm sorry. We don't have enough in common. I wish you luck finding a match."

"I can like new things. Please meet me."

"I'm sorry. No."

"Really. I think you'll like me once you meet me."

"I'm sorry. No."

"Give me your number and I'll call you. I'll change your mind. I'm sure of it."

Annoyed, I typed, "No."

A week passed.

He contacted me again. "I see you're still on here. You haven't found anyone yet because you're supposed to be with me."

"Please stop contacting me. I'm not interested."

"I'm very interesting in person. You will love me. I'm sure of it."

"No. Please do not contact me again. I don't want to report you."

"You will regret not meeting me."

I was regretting ever responding to him in the first place. He kept contacting me. But I did not respond to any more of his messages. I eventually reported him because he would not stop e-mailing me.

Bachelor #10 was 42 years old and worked in the entertainment industry. I agreed to meet him for a drink. He looked much different in person. And he lied about having animals. His shirt was covered with cat hair. So, I sat as far away as I could and popped some Benadryl.

I honestly can not tell you what we talked about. I was too preoccupied with the appearance of his leathery skin. He must have spent every minute of every day in the sun, baking himself until extra crispy. And his mannerisms were beyond quirky. I kept thinking he looked and acted reptilian, like a *Star Trek* character.

I drank most of my drink. I just wanted to get out of there. As I got up to leave, he tried to hug me. I pushed him away. He looked hurt.

Annoyed, I blurted, "You're covered in cat hair. I told you I was severely allergic to animals."

He replied, "I can fix that."

Then, he did the unthinkable. He took off his shirt.

So there he was—standing there in a white, "wife-beater" T-shirt. His scrawny, over-tanned body was covered with ugly, disturbing black tattoos. And I mean *covered*.

I rolled my eyes and shook my head. "Put your clothes back on."

"But ..."

Exasperated, I said, "Sorry. I'm going home. Thanks for the drink." And I walked away.

He actually had the nerve to contact me for another date.

Oh, hell no!

Then there were the bachelors who felt it necessary to send pictures of themselves. Yes, I am talking about *those* kind of pictures. *Why? Why? Why?*

Why do men think it is appropriate to send strangers pictures of their genitalia? I do not, I repeat, I do not want to see these pictures.

I know politicians do it all the time. But these guys are not politicians. And I am sorry to say, these men did not have anything impressive to be exposing in the first place.

My computer felt dirty after viewing those pictures. I really wanted to wipe off the screen with Lysol antibacterial wipes. Just even thinking about it now makes me want to clean something.

Worst Pickup Lines Ever

My girlfriends and I enjoy drama-free girls' nights out. However, inevitably, we are approached by less-than-desirable men looking for a good time. Here were the worst lines we heard recently.

10) My buddy and I noticed you from across the bar. I really love your spangly bracelets.

Sure, it was my spangly bracelets that caught his attention. Not. I was wearing an outfit similar to one I wore for my professional photo shoot. I had the romantic vibe going, including soft waves in my hair, flawless makeup, and a hint of cleavage. Needless to say, after we stopped laughing, we sent him on his merry way. I gave him points for effort and creativity!

9) I think we would make beautiful music together.

Not really a bad line, in and of itself. But when a guy old enough to be your father, wearing a zoot suit, delivers it, it is just creepy.

"No, thank you. You're not my type."

"What's your type?"

I wanted to say, "Someone who's not my father's age." Instead, I rattled off a list.

He protested, "I don't like what's on your list."

"You don't have to. It's my list."

"There are a lot of things missing from your list." Then, he proceeded to tell me the attributes that should have been on my list.

I reiterated that I was not interested, but he would not leave. Thankfully, within moments, I was saved. He had signed up to sing karaoke, and he was up. Thank you, God!

8) How'd you get that scar on your neck? Did you have a tracheotomy?

What a jerk!

"No, I had cancer. Great way to start and end a first conversation."

7) Nice jeans.

Attention, ladies! This is a "politically correct" way for a guy to tell you that you have a nice ass. Apparently, it replaced the wolf whistle and other direct commentary that could be construed as sexual harassment. I did not bother to acknowledge his presence. To tell the truth, they were nice jeans. Actually, they were my favorite jeans.

6) My friend and I have a bet going. Are those real?

Seriously?

Stunned by his audacity, I redirected, "Yes, my eyes are this color. I'm not wearing colored contacts."

"That's not what I meant."

"I know. But that's the only answer you're getting."

5) You're hot. I'm hot. Let's f***.

Are you kidding me?

"Oh, hell no!" Picture me rolling my eyes and shaking my head in total and absolute disgust.

4) What are you drinking?

Okay, the question was not the problem here, it was the conversation that followed that did him in.

Lifting my drink, I said, "Ginger ale with cranberry juice."

He laughed and replied, "I want to buy you a real drink. Order something strong."

"Nope. This is what I'm drinking. I already had my one alcoholic drink for the evening. I'm the designated driver."

"That's ridiculous."

"No."

"Come on. I want to talk to you."

Incredulous, I replied, "And you can't talk to me unless I'm drinking alcohol? That's pretty pathetic."

"It levels the playing field."

"I'm not interested in playing games. Go away, and grow up."

3) You girls are gorgeous. Have you ever considered doing porn?

This guy approached us from behind and put one arm around each of us. We immediately pulled away and told him to get away from us. *Eeewww!* No matter how hard we tried, no amount of antibacterial wipes made us feel clean after that.

2) I'm a single dad with four kids under the age of five. I'm looking for somebody to raise them for me.

Well, good luck with that!

While we laughed, he explained he liked to cruise around on his motorcycle. He was searching for someone to raise his kids for him, so he could gallivant around the country. We suggested he hire a nanny.

1) I loved *50 Shades of Grey*. How about you?

Without having to think, I responded, "Hated it."

"How could you hate it? It was fantastic."

"The plot was ridiculous. It was poorly written and 200 pages too long."

"Come back to my place, and I'll convince you otherwise."

"I can't say, 'No,' strongly enough."

"I'll have you saying, 'Yes,' and begging for more."

"Not in your wildest dreams."

"I guarantee to make your wildest dreams come true."

"Really?"

"Yes."

"My wildest dream is for you to leave us alone."

And with that, he called me the "B" word and left.

Gee, if only all of my dreams were that easy to fulfill!

Searching For Mrs. Robinson

The subjects for this entry are younger than most. Initially, I wanted to call this, "Hot for Teacher." But the more I wrote, the more I liked, "Searching for Mrs. Robinson."

You could tell Bachelor #11 was trouble by his profile picture—an all-American boy with a mischievous twinkle in his eye. You know the kind—trouble with a capital "T." I refer to him as a "boy" because he was a 24-year-old college student. Technically, I am old enough to be his mother.

He wrote, "Came across your photo. Couldn't resist. Please give me your number."

"Sorry, but I think you should look for someone more age appropriate."

He replied, "I don't mind. Give me your number."

"Well, I do mind. You should find someone your own age."

"No, you're what I'm looking for. You'd make a good teacher, I bet."

What is it about younger guys wanting teachers? "I'm not interested in teaching you anything, except for, possibly, manners."

"That sounds kinky. Give me your number."

Sheesh. "I wasn't trying to be coy. I'm not interested. Good luck finding a match."

"What's coy?"

"Find a dictionary, and look it up."

"Are you a librarian? Do you wear those tight skirts and your hair up? I'd like that."

I'm sure you would. "I'm not interested. Good luck finding a match."

Next up was Bachelor #12, a 35-year-old consultant.

His e-mail began innocently enough. "How are you? I am hesitant to reach out to you. Mainly because I am putting myself in a position to be ridiculed and/or rejected. But, my hope is that you will respect my candor and honesty, as opposed to being offended."

Intrigued, I answered, "Well, you haven't offended me yet. And I appreciate candor and honesty. So, go ahead."

He continued, "I really haven't been very active in the dating scene and/or on this site. So, I found myself wondering 'why am I on this site?' the other day. I truly couldn't answer that question, lol. However, I think I've realized that I want something new, exciting, and…not boring. I want to meet a woman at least 5 years outside of my age bracket, who is interested in a professional, vibrant, intellectual, witty, younger man."

"You have piqued my interest. I don't mind dating a younger man. So, that's not an issue. And I definitely agree that a relationship should be exciting, not boring."

"Now, here's the catch. I'm not wanting a serious relationship. Not dead-set against it, but just not prioritizing it. I am very focused on my career and have goals to accomplish (just as you do, I'm sure). In all honesty, I'd love to meet a woman who craves and desires a younger man…even if she's never been with one. I have a feeling that 'older' women appreciate a younger man's intimacy, so long as he is energetic, passionate, and unselfish….oh, and privy to what will make her feel 'euphoric'. Actually, that last one should probably be a pre-req for both sides, lol."

Euphoric? Well, who wouldn't want to feel euphoric? And when was the last time any man wanted to make me happy, let alone euphoric?

I reread his reply again, just to make sure I understood him clearly. But, then I got distracted by the whole "energetic, passionate, unselfish" bit. If any woman deserved a man who was energetic, passionate, and unselfish, it was me. Visions of satin sheets, rose petals, and candles flooded my mind. Then, I read it again for good measure.

I had to admit that was the best soliloquy I've read that boiled down to, "I just want to have sex. And I promise you'll enjoy it."

While I attempted to entertain the idea of this euphoric opportunity for a split second, my mother's voice screamed in my head, loud and clear. "Are you crazy? Have you completely lost your mind?"

Fear not, Mom. I want to be in a serious relationship, not be some young stud's booty call. And in all honesty, I did not want to endure the inevitable, extremely awkward lecture from my mother.

So, you're asking, "Why on earth would you tell your mother?"

I wouldn't have to *tell* anybody. If Mr. Booty Call lived up to expectations, I am guessing everyone who saw me or spoke to me would notice my new, improved blissful state of being. You know that state—you are floating on air, the sun is always shining, and everything is happiness, butterflies, and rainbows.

Okay, maybe it wouldn't be exactly like that. Although, it might be worth it to test my theory! (Just kidding, Mom.)

Anyway ...

I wrote back to Mr. Booty Call. "I am flattered. But I am not interested in that type of relationship. However, I must compliment you on how eloquently you expressed the bottom line. I'm sure there is a woman out there who will be happy to oblige."

"I sincerely apologize if I've offended you."

"You didn't offend me. Dating sites aren't for the faint of heart. I wish you luck finding a match."

"Thank you. I wish you all the best on this site and in your other dating endeavors."

Unlucky Bachelor #13 was a self-proclaimed virgin at the age of 30. He was a computer specialist. I know, cliché. But it gets even worse, so keep reading.

He wrote, "I would be honored if you would be my Padmé Amidala to my Anakin Skywalker."

Heavy sigh. "Sorry, but Anakin becomes Darth Vader. And I don't feel like fighting any wars against the Dark Side. I wish you the best and may The Force be with you."

"You could be Princess Leia. I could be Han Solo."

He did not have a picture posted. Unfortunately, at this point, I'm imagining he's probably more like Jabba the Hutt, and I have a strong aversion to chains. I also would not be caught dead with a pair of Cinnabons covering my ears. "I'm sorry, no. I wish you luck in finding a match."

"I'll be anyone you want me to be. Just name it. I have an awesome costume collection."

Oh, dear. I'm sure you do.

I pitied this kid. "I am not interested. However, in the future, when contacting other women, I suggest that you be yourself. Save the characters for later."

"OK. Thanks."

Call me old-fashioned, but I think you should know the guy's name and perhaps meet him in person before delving into role-playing fantasies and discovering whatever else he's hiding in his closet. This poor guy was going to need the full power of The Force behind him to find a woman.

Oh ladies! I wish I could include Bachelor #14's picture. In his profile picture, he was impeccably dressed in a classic black tuxedo. That 28-year-old could have had a spread in, GQ, or any other magazine his heart desired. He was absolutely, positively gorgeous and quite the catch for someone. He reminded me of Shemar Moore. For those of you not familiar with Shemar, he exuded his undeniable and irresistible hotness on, *The Young and the Restless*, *Criminal Minds*, and *Diary of a Mad Black Woman*.

Mmm mmm! What I wouldn't do for a man like Shemar Moore. He's a perfect example of a man who qualifies as a gift from heaven. From his beautifully toned body, to his sexy swagger, to the smoothness of his voice ... Whoops! Where was I?

Oh yeah, Bachelor #14. An MBA was not enough for him. He was now pursuing a law degree.

He opened, "I would love the opportunity to speak with you."

Why couldn't you be ten years older?

Disappointed, I replied, "Thank you. But I think I'm too old for you."

"Please don't dismiss me yet. I am looking for a mature woman. I'm not interested in needy, clingy girls. I'm looking for a woman who I can have stimulating ..."

Oh geez. Here we go.

He finished his thought, "Conversations. I'm looking for a woman who I can have stimulating conversations with. Sorry. My finger slipped and it sent before I was finished."

Good recovery.

"I like intelligent conversations on a variety of subjects. I'm looking for a sophisticated woman who can hold her own and would make a good impression at black tie events, law firm events, symposiums, etc. You seem to have a wide range of interests, you're educated and you're very attractive. I need someone like you by my side."

Searching for smart arm candy, are you? Now that's something that would be great on a resumé—Intelligent Arm Candy, well-versed in a variety of topics.

I typed, "Thank you. But this sounds more like a job than a romantic relationship. I am not the right woman for you."

"I'd like to object. I believe you are."

Wow! You objected?

Flabbergasted that he objected, I responded, "Sorry, you're overruled. We are at different stages in our lives. Trust me. I know what I'm talking about. This is not open to debate. I wish you well."

"Thank you for your time. Best of luck to you."

At this point, I'll take luck or The Force. Whichever works more quickly ...

The Old Bait and Switch

You hear men complain about women who post old pictures of themselves on dating sites. Well, I'm here to tell you, men do it too.

Although I usually go for the nerdy type, I decided to throw caution to the wind and give Bachelor #15, a professional athlete, a try.

He sent me a poem about rose petals and the morning dew. I gave him kudos for the effort and agreed to meet him.

His profile stated he was 48 years old and a non-smoker. The pictures might have been from when he was 48, but he ended up being 58. And he definitely smoked. Why smokers think they can hide their smoking from non-smokers, I will never know. We know. We *always* know.

I asked why he lied about his age.

He answered, "Would you have agreed to meet me if I said I was 58?"

"Honestly, no."

"That's why I lied."

"Well, unfortunately, that makes me wonder what else you're lying about. You lied about smoking too."

"So, you have trust issues?"

"Only with people who lie to me."

Defensively, he responded, "Everybody lies."

I disagreed, "No, not everybody does."

"You're kidding yourself. Everybody lies."

I elaborated, "I'm talking about important things. There's a big difference between telling a friend her butt doesn't look big in her new dress when you're already at a cocktail party and lying about facts, like your age, if you smoke, and if you're really divorced."

"I am divorced."

"So, one out of three isn't bad in your book?"

He smirked.

"What if I had done the same to you?"

He appeared annoyed with my question.

I persisted, "Seriously. What if I showed up and was ten years older than I said I was?"

He muttered, "I'd be pissed."

"There you go! So, you don't like to be lied to either."

He tossed back the remainder of his drink. "I'm not getting laid tonight, am I?"

Shaking my head in disbelief, I replied, "Not unless you pick up someone on a corner on your way home."

On that note, he got up, threw some cash on the table to cover our drinks, and left.

The next contender was a salesman who advertised his age as 49. He turned out to be 54. The ironic thing was that he looked better in person. A lot better.

I inquired, "Why don't you have a more current picture posted?"

Smiling, he answered, "I figure if someone likes me heavier and with gray hair, then they'll like me thinner with darker hair."

"So, it's like a test?"

"Yes."

Leery, I said, "Interesting."

"Interesting good or interesting bad?"

"The jury's still out."

"You're funny."

I was not attempting to be funny. I was trying to figure him out. So, I asked him to tell me about himself.

Big mistake. He droned on and on about all of the "important people" he knew. He dropped so many names that I tripped over them. Noticeably, there were not any stories about doing anything with them.

My theory was that he hangs out at St. Elmo's on big event nights and introduces himself to everyone who walks in the door. That would explain how he "knows" the rich and famous. (St. Elmo Steak House is a world-renowned restaurant, in Indianapolis, which made Forbes' list of "10 Great Classic Restaurants Well Worth Visiting.")

When he wasn't bragging about the people he knew, he pointed out his designer clothes and how he only wore the very best. He proceeded to list all of his favorite designers and stores.

Okay, I'll admit that I watch *Project Runway*. I'm familiar with high-end designers and fashion. I own a few nice designer items. But I don't talk about them.

This guy never got around to asking me much of anything. The jury's verdict is in: Guilty of being a boastful, materialistic, narcissistic jerk.

Bachelor #17 was a 46-year-old entrepreneur who owned multiple residences in several states. At 99%, we were almost a perfect match, according to the dating site's algorithm. His pictures showed a thin, handsome man, with a full head of black wavy hair, and a smile that would knock you over.

No coffee or drinks for this guy. He went straight for dinner.

A girl has to eat, so I agreed.

As I entered the restaurant, I searched for the dashing man in the pictures. Imagine my surprise when instead, I was greeted by an 80-pound heavier Mr. Comb-Over. The smile was still there. Thank God for small favors.

After chatting for a few minutes, he revealed that his pictures were ten years old. All I thought about was shaving his head. The comb-over look is wrong on any man. Period.

Our date went well. He was easy to talk to, and we had no shortage of topics to discuss. At the end of the evening, he insisted on buying my books. I signed copies for him, and we agreed on a second date.

The second date went just as nicely as the first. He gushed over my poetry book. He even started quoting some of my work. How refreshing—a man taking a genuine interest in me.

After that date, he started reciting other people's poetry to me over the phone. Then the texts started. Lots of texts. Late at night.

First, it was rambling poetry. Then, it morphed into sexting. Obsessive sexting. I told him to stop. He didn't. His sexting became more graphic. It was disturbing.

I told him I was done and not to contact me again. He was hurt and did not understand why.

I did not want to upset this obsessive, stalker kind of guy. Therefore, I told him he reminded me of my ex-husband and left it at that.

He bought my story and left me alone. Thank you, God!

Bachelor #18 was a doctor. We were the same age. According to my computer, we were a 100% match. Imagine my mom's reaction being something like, "Oh, a doctor! I hope this one works out."

The doctor and I chatted on the phone and agreed to meet for coffee. Since I don't drink coffee, I ordered hot chocolate.

He was shier than I had anticipated and wore a Panama Jack-style hat that he never removed. A wee bit eccentric, perhaps. But I'm used to eccentric. The conversation went pretty well, but he had to leave after an hour. We agreed to meet again.

The next time, it was for a drink. And again, for exactly one hour. My instincts told me something was rotten in Denmark.

Sure enough, I was right. After some relentless questioning, he admitted he was not divorced. He was meeting with me when he should have been watching his son play soccer.

Slime ball.

That really irked me. "So, you're a liar, a cheater, and a lousy father? What a sad excuse of a man you are. You're despicable."

Angrily, he questioned, "And I guess you're little Miss Perfect?"

"I'll be the first one to admit that I'm not perfect. But I don't tolerate cheating, and I don't date married men."

I wished that my glass had been full. I could have made a dramatic exit by throwing the contents in his face and storming out. Alas, there was not a drop remaining. So, I just grabbed my purse and left.

Bachelor #19's profile indicated he lived in Indianapolis. After a pleasant phone call, he asked to meet somewhere around South Bend.

Confused, I said, "That's almost three hours away. We can wait until you're back in town to get together."

He confessed, "Um, I live in Chicago."

"Your profile says you live in Indy."

"Yeah, I can't find anyone nice in Chicago."

"Chicago is a huge city. And it has tons of suburbs. I think you need to try a little harder to find someone in your area."

"Nope. I've looked. There isn't anybody."

Red flag! If this guy couldn't find someone in all of Chicago and the surrounding areas, something was wrong with him. "I'm sorry, but I don't do long distance relationships."

"You could move up here. I've got a nice place. You could stay with me."

Not on your life, buddy. I watch CSI *and* Criminal Minds. "I'm not going anywhere. Good luck to you."

A 28-year-old salesman was lonely Bachelor #20. His profile stated he lived in Dayton, OH.

He typed, "I'd like to meet you for coffee sometime."

"Sorry, I don't do long distance relationships."

"I live in Castleton, IN."

"So, do you work in Dayton?"

"I work in Indy."

Scratching my head, I asked, "If you live in Castleton and work in Indy, why are you saying you live in Dayton?"

"I don't want my coworkers to see me on here."

"Why? If they're on here too, what's the big deal?"

"Idk. I'm embarrassed." (Idk is "I don't know" for you non-texting readers.)

"That makes no sense. There's no reason to be embarrassed. You need to update your city, or you are never going to find a match."

"I'm afraid they'll make fun of me."

Wow, kid. You need to grow a set.

"Forget about your coworkers. If they make fun of you, they're not your friends. Change your city."

"I'll think about it."

This kid needed guidance. I felt compelled to provide it. "You need to surround yourself with positive, supportive people. You need to do something to boost your self-confidence, or you're going to get eaten alive out there. That pertains to your business and personal relationships. Whatever your story, you need to get your head on straight. It will make a world of difference."

"You seem nice and smart. Will you meet me?"

"No. You're too young anyway. Change your city, and hang out with positive people."

"Thx."

"You're welcome. Best of luck."

The more dates and interactions I have, I realize that I should have gone into psychology. These guys need professional help.

Here's some free advice for everyone—be honest. It *is* the best policy.

Doctors & Chemists & A Cowboy, Oh My!

I am sure you're wondering if I met a doctor who made house calls, or if I developed an organic relationship with a chemist, or if the cowboy was a stripper or an actual cowboy. There's only one way to answer those questions. Read on!

Perhaps it was time to have a doctor in the family. Hopeful #21 was a 45-year-old anesthesiologist. We met for coffee. He was handsome and dressed like a professional golfer. But he showed up late. And he didn't bother to text or call to let me know. A lady does not like to be kept waiting.

Strike one.

He asked me what I wanted to drink and got in line to order. When he returned, he had more than drinks. He purchased brunch. For himself. He did not offer me any food. He sat there eating in front of me.

Strike two.

The conversation was less than stimulating. I actually think he could save hospitals money on anesthesia and sedatives by just talking to patients. Major snooze fest.

He asked how long I had been divorced. I told him several months.

I bounced the question back to him. He responded he wasn't divorced. It was going to be too expensive. He was weighing his options.

Well, I eliminated one option for him—me.

Strike three. He's out!

Bachelor #22 was 50 years old and a surgeon. Another coffee date. I guess doctors love their coffee. However, this one arrived on time, in a black Mercedes. He had a certain air about him as he walked in. As we shook hands, I noticed his bling. Hard to miss it—thick gold chain around his neck, ostentatious rings, and a gold Rolex watch.

But as the Shania Twain song goes, "That don't impress me much." Sorry, but I'm more concerned with what's inside a man's head and heart than a flashy outer package. It always makes me wonder if they're overcompensating for something.

I sensed a God complex as soon as he started talking about his grand achievements. Don't get me wrong, I admire people who accomplish great things. I just didn't like how he bragged about them. Plus the fact that he was not interested in me.

When I told him that I had published a romance novel and a poetry book, I got *that* look. It's the, "Oh, you're an artsy, fartsy type" look. I hate that look.

It didn't last long. He switched the conversation back to him. He loved to hear himself talk. I admired his perfect manicure as he chattered on.

Fortunately, he had to get to the office. I never heard from him again. No loss there.

Fifty-three-year-old potential suitor #23 was a gastroenterologist. Some of my family members were thrilled at the idea of having one of those around. My sister-in-law even told me that it did not matter what he was like, I should "take one for the team."

Can you feel the love?

We met for drinks and shared vacation stories. His international vacation tales were genuinely interesting. I mentally made a bucket list of places to visit in the future.

For those of you who know me, you know I only drink one drink if I will be driving later. One. Count it. One.

He suggested, "Have another drink."

"No, thank you. I only drink one drink."

"Oh, come on. Have another."

"No, thank you." *No means no!*

He yelled to the bartender, "Another drink for the lady."

I looked at the bartender. "I don't want another drink. Can I have some water?"

The doctor insisted, "Give her another drink."

"Don't bother. I won't drink it."

Well, I ended up with the water and another drink.

After a few minutes, the doctor complained, "You haven't touched your drink."

"I told you that I wouldn't."

"What's the big deal?"

"It's not a big deal. But you're making it one. When I say I'm not going to do something, I mean it."

"It's just one drink."

I sensed a major control problem. "I'm not drinking it."

"You should."

"No. Thank you for the drink that I did order. It's time to call it a night."

He continued to contact me afterward. I told him to move on.

Anyone who was that obsessed over getting me to drink something that I didn't want to drink has serious control issues. I can not even imagine what he would be like concerning important things.

I met Bachelor #24, an R&D Chemist, for dinner. The 50-year-old was interesting, on paper. In person, I felt as if I was conducting an audit.

If you have never been prepped for an audit, Rule #1 is: Stick to the facts. Rule #2 is: Do not elaborate.

It was like pulling teeth. Some answers were one word. Others came in sentence form. Short sentences. I ended up talking most of the time because he wouldn't.

At least the food was really good. And I had leftovers for the next night. So, it wasn't a total waste of time.

I gave another chemist a try. Number 25 picked the same restaurant as the last one. I wasn't sure if that was a good thing or not. Nevertheless, I knew the food would be good. So, I met the 42-year-old for dinner.

This guy never shut up. It was all negative stuff about his ex-wife. The language he used was downright ugly. It was offensive to me as a woman. Granted, she might have been exactly as he described her. But I did not want to hear it. I was certain the couple behind him did not want to hear it. The woman kept giving me looks. She even followed me into the bathroom.

Standing in front of the sinks, she stated, "That guy you're with is a jackass."

"Agreed. It's a first date."

"Hopefully your last too."

"Yes. As soon as the check is paid, I'm out of here."

"I'd leave now if I were you. Slip out the back door."

I laughed. "My sweater is on my chair."

"I'd forget the sweater. Leave now."

"It's a really nice sweater. It took me forever to find it."

"Suit yourself."

Luckily, he paid the check while I was powdering my nose. I invented a friend emergency and made a quick exit.

Gather around the campfire for Bachelor #26. I do not know what it is about cowboys that intrigues us women. Maybe it's the rugged look about them. Or the fact that they seem to be able to handle any problem that arises better than MacGyver. Or perhaps it's that they have manners and tip their hats. Or maybe it's just the tight jeans.

His ultimate passion was his ranch. Although, this 50-year-old cowboy had a real job during the day. Our phone conversation was so exhilarating; I violated my "no pets" rule. The tone of his voice was incredible. I had to meet the man on the other end of the phone, despite the fact that he had dogs and horses.

Ladies, he did not disappoint. This rugged, clean-shaven hunk of a man wore a black, fitted cowboy shirt to highlight his toned upper half. His jeans were broken in in all the right places. And his boots were polished nicely.

Big & Rich's song, "Save A Horse [Ride A Cowboy]," played in my head.

Oh, my goodness! Is it hot in here or just me?

He was absolutely fascinating. The hours flew by. We were the last people in the restaurant. The waiter vacuumed around us. We took that as our cue to leave. It was a delightful evening.

As a gentleman should, he walked me to my car. He leaned in, gave me a quick hug and kiss, and he was on his way.

As I watched him walk to his car, my throat started closing up. I grabbed two Benadryl and my emergency meds out of my purse and swallowed them all quickly. I drove toward home (and the hospital), Epi-pen in hand. Just in case.

The coughing and wheezing subsided after about thirty minutes. At least I didn't have to use the Epi-pen, and I didn't end up in the ER.

It also meant that no matter how fantastic he was, or how well we got along, or how good he looked in those jeans, there was no chance of a relationship with this man.

I told him the news. He said that he regretted not kissing me deeply. Dear Lord, if he had, I have no doubt that I would have ended up in the hospital. Although, that would have made one heck of a story.

I'm Not Like Other Guys

Bachelor #27 and I shared so many interests, it was unbelievable. Every line I read, I smiled and nodded my head. And no pets! The computer screen told me that we were a 100% match! Could this be possible? After all I had been through already, I hoped, and I prayed.

I will not reveal his age or profession for reasons that will become clear as you read on. Actually, the original blog post was censored. However, I decided to tell the entire story in this book.

After a few e-mail exchanges, we spoke on the phone. His voice was velvety smooth, an easy listening radio voice for sure. That first phone conversation lasted two hours. It felt like mere minutes.

During our first dinner date, he displayed impeccable manners and was very complimentary to me. Did I mention that he was dashing and handsome?

We had similar hobbies and the exact same taste in music. He was also a muscle car guy. A GM muscle car guy. Thank God he wasn't a Ford or Chrysler guy. (No offense to Ford or Chrysler guys, but I know GM cars. I don't know squat about the others.)

An unprecedented month of dates followed. We enjoyed each other's company tremendously.

Then one evening, he said, "We need to talk."

Oh crap. Nothing good ever follows those words. I braced myself.

"There's something I need to tell you."

Maybe his ex's name is tattooed on him somewhere. Or he's a convicted felon. A serial killer. Bodies buried in the backyard. I could be next. Mom was right! Or he's married. Or an illegal alien. Or he works for the Mob. Or worse, he liked, "50 Shades of Grey."

"I've wanted to tell you for some time now."

"Okay. I'm listening."

"I'm not like other guys."

At that moment, I flashed back to the beginning of Michael Jackson's, *Thriller*, video. Those were the words Michael said to his date before he turned into the werewolf. Oh crap.

He stood up and removed the top of his jogging outfit. What I saw stunned me. He stood before me wearing a lacy bra.

I was speechless. Utterly. Totally. Speechless. For the first time in my life, I had no words. None.

The worst part about it was what I was thinking. The bra was the wrong size. Honestly, he needed a bigger size.

This man who I thought could be, "The One," was standing in front of me in a lacy bra. Picture me sitting there stunned. Really stunned. Deer-in-the-headlights stunned.

Hopefully, my mouth wasn't hanging open. I don't remember, but it's fully in the realm of possibility.

He took my silence to be acceptance and started to push his pants down.

I held up my hand. "No! Stop!"

I saw the lacy top of the panties. I did not want to see any more. I knew once I saw him standing there in a bra and matching panties, I could never unsee it.

My mind attempted to process the situation. So many questions raced through my mind.

He got dressed. "Say something."

The unfortunate question that popped out of my mouth: "Does this mean you play for both teams?"

Disappointed, he answered, "No. I'm straight."

"Okay." Meaning, okay, I heard him, but I still didn't know what to think.

He stated, "I love wearing women's lingerie. I love the feel of it."

I offered, "You can feel it if I'm wearing it."

"No. I need to be the one wearing it, especially during sex."

He explained how this fetish started when he was young. He also loved wearing women's clothing. He expressed an interest in sharing my clothing and lingerie.

I don't think so. If he wore my clothes and lingerie, he would stretch them out in all the wrong places. And I refuse to share underwear with anyone. I draw the line there. My underwear is *my* underwear.

I want to make it clear that I do not have a problem with cross-dressing. However, the idea of being intimate with a man who's wearing my lingerie does not turn me on at all.

He said, "Think about it."

There was no doubt in my mind. That's all I would be thinking about in the near future. The question remained, "Could I live with it?"

I thought long and hard about it for a couple of days. I researched it on the Internet. There were psychological explanations and justifications. All articles agreed it was a harmless practice. Apparently, it's more common than any of us would ever have imagined.

I finally made my decision. I could not live with it. I wanted to. He was a great guy, otherwise. We had so much in common. He treated me beautifully. Everything had been falling into place. But I could not live with that one thing. It was too big. And he was not willing to give it up.

So, that was the end of our relationship.

When I told my mother I broke up with him, she couldn't believe it. "What was wrong with this one? You said he was perfect."

"He had a fetish."

"Oh my God! Oh my God! Don't tell me!"

"But …"

She was adamant. "No, don't tell me! I don't want to know what it is."

"It's not horrible. I just couldn't live with it. It's not like he murders people or anything."

"No! Don't say it! I don't want to have nightmares!"

"But …"

"No! Don't tell me!"

So, I didn't tell her. I did not want to be responsible for giving my mother nightmares. She loses so much sleep worrying about me to begin with, when she does fall asleep, I don't want it to be nightmares about fetishes.

I don't want anyone he knows to find out either. It's not like he broadcasted this to his family, friends, and co-workers. He was a nice guy. It just didn't work out.

In the meantime, not knowing was driving my mother crazy. She started guessing.

I laughed. "I thought you didn't want to know what it was."

"I changed my mind. Was he a crossdresser?"

"Yes. He wanted to wear my clothes and lingerie. And he would have to wear women's lingerie when we were intimate in order for him to enjoy it."

"Ick. Now I understand why you broke up with him."

I am pleased to report he found someone, and they got married. I am happy he found the right woman. I wish them all the best.

A Motherly Type of Love

I decided to stop numbering my potential suitors. It's becoming depressing. From now on, there will only be nameless, numberless men.

I dated the next guy for several months. He was a well-built military veteran, a few years my junior. He had a good job. That is all I can say about it. If I told you what it was, I'd have to kill you. At least that's what he kept telling me.

He was chatty and had lots of exciting stories to share. He expressed an interest in moving out of Indiana. Fine with me. He even eagerly embraced my antibacterial wipes! Actually, he touched less things than I would. To alleviate stress, he liked to clean. That was a win/win in my book!

I introduced him to my family and some friends. Those encounters went well, except for the raking incident with my dad. Dad didn't know he was behind him and ended up ramming the end of the rake into his face. Nothing says, "Nice to meet you," like a black eye on Thanksgiving. Anyway …

As time progressed, he faced difficult challenges. Night terrors and panic attacks were frequent. Physically, his war injuries were increasingly causing severe, and often debilitating, mobility issues. He had difficulty performing daily tasks.

I accompanied him to his VA appointments, in an attempt to learn more, so I could help him. However, I was ill-prepared when he experienced a psychotic episode while we were at a restaurant waiting for dinner. He thought we were in battle and under fire. He insisted we had to take cover and plan our escape.

I had to think quickly. I had to keep him calm while trying not to terrify everyone around us. Not trained for this type of scenario, I treated him like a sleep-walker. I went along with the story as I guided him out of the building to the safety of my car. He felt claustrophobic in the car, so I drove like a bat out of hell to get him home. There, I reassured him he was safe, and it was time to rest. I told him to sleep while I kept watch. And watch, I did.

I prayed that when he awakened, the episode would be over. God answered my prayers. When he awoke, he was grounded in reality.

After that, I ended up serving more as a mother than a girlfriend. I read everything I could to understand PTSD. It became a full-time job to manage his day-to-day activities. It was physically and mentally exhausting. I struggled. While attempting to help him, I was killing myself in the process. I was not properly equipped to handle this intense level of stress. I ended up having daily panic attacks.

I knew that I would be a motherly-type figure in a caretaker role forever. That was not what either of us wanted or deserved. With a heavy heart, I told him I could not handle the situation any longer. We had to go our separate ways.

It was the right thing to do. However, the guilt weighed on me. The VA failed to take care of him properly when he returned home. Now, I failed him too.

The Foreign Contingent

The bachelors in this excerpt were all born outside of the United States. Indiana's state motto is: "The Crossroads of America." Apparently, we are creating quite the melting pot in Indianapolis. Diversity is a good thing for Honest-to-Goodness Indiana. If you know me, you know I love learning about new cultures and traditions.

I probably should have mentioned this earlier, but the men that you're reading about are from all different backgrounds, religions, and ethnicities. For the most part, I do not specify a bachelor's ethnicity unless it is somehow relevant to the story. Throughout this journey, I went on dates with men with every skin tone under the sun.

Many of you also know that my ex-husband was Indian. His family was from the Punjab region in India. Yes, we had an Indian Sikh wedding. Anyway ...

Getting back to my story, I was contacted by men who were originally from fourteen different countries, including India, Pakistan, Greece, Lebanon, Iran, England, Japan, and Canada.

Somehow, I attracted all of the Indian men within a fifty-mile radius. And 99% of them were doctors. Amazingly enough, they were deep into poetry and spirituality. As a poet, that intrigued me, because most men are not keen on poetry.

The conversations were interesting, enlightening, and intellectual. One of the men was even Punjabi. He was thrilled beyond belief that I knew what that meant. However, there was an element lacking with each and every one—chemistry.

Moving on to merry old England. The phone conversation with the English guy was awful. He was crass and rude. I started fantasizing about my own version of, *My Fair Lady*. I would be a kind professor teaching this brute of a man how to become a real gentleman.

The Iranian hopeful, a self-advertised non-smoker, had a smoker's cough so bad, I thought he would cough up a lung during our phone conversation. I felt compelled to lecture him on the dangers of smoking. But that would have required me to listen to him cough longer. Ugh.

The Pakistani bachelor seemed nice on the phone, but I could not understand him most of the time. He sent me pictures of flowers. It was his way of giving me flowers. Sweet. But I did not grant him a live date. I knew I would have spent the entire night asking him to repeat himself. That would not have been enjoyable for either of us.

The Greek candidate passed the phone interview. In person, he was gorgeous—perfect olive complexion, thick black curly hair, and a smile that made me melt. He walked with confidence and had a magnificent personality. But alas, he wanted babies. Lots and lots of babies.

Why does God hate me? Why?

Then there was the bachelor from Japan. His introductory e-mail read: "Hello! Have you traveled to Japan? What kind of cooking do you like? Do you like sushi?"

My mind answered quickly, "No, I haven't. The kind of cooking someone else does. Sushi? I love sushi, but way to stereotype yourself." *Sheesh.*

His height was listed as 5'1". I'm almost 5'7". I don't wear flats. Even my flip-flops are wedges. Talk about an odd couple. With my lowest heels being two inches, we would be eight inches different in height. He would look like my child, not my date. That would be all sorts of wrong.

The Lebanese bachelor was great on the phone. In person, he was boorish and drank like a fish. I stopped counting after six mixed drinks in less than an hour and a half. I would have left sooner, but it took forever to get the food. Hey, I had to eat.

Then, he refused to walk me to my car. I had parked four blocks away down a side street. He opted to stay and drink some more. I power-walked to my car, in the dark. The side street had no lights. Luckily, I made it in one piece. The only redeeming feature of the night was the food.

The French-Canadian guy took the cake. Period. Hands down winner.

"I would love to get to know you more better and see how it goes between us, I am mixed race, Dad Canada, Mum America. I lived in Canada all my life."

I laughed as I read it. But based on the rest of the e-mail, I knew he was serious about the "mixed race" part. After the initial e-mail exchange, he revealed that he was working in Africa. He would require me to move to Canada as soon as possible to help raise his young son.

Move to Canada? To raise his son while he's in Africa? Um, no!

I quickly typed, "I'm sorry, but long distance relationships don't work for me. I wish you luck finding a match."

I figured that would be the end of that. *Au contraire, mes amis.*

"I quite understand how you mean but I seriously do not see distance as a barrier in a relationship in as much as true love and affection till the end of time."

"I'm sorry, no."

"I believe things happen for a reason, a connection happens when the right person comes."

"I'm sorry. I will not move to Canada. I am not the right person for you."

"Just thought it would be a nice idea to know some things about each other, it will be my pleasure to get to know more about you and answer the following love questions."

There were thirty-eight "love questions" that followed. *Thirty-eight!*

There were basic questions, such as, "What do you seek in a relationship?" But there were slightly ambiguous questions, such as, "Do you like public intimacy?"

I wasn't sure if he was asking about public displays of affection or if I liked having sex in public places.

The very last question on his "love questions" list was, "Would you hit your man for any reason?"

I wanted to answer, "Yes, if he repeatedly ignored every word I said and sent me a list of thirty-eight 'love questions' to answer even though I'm clearly not interested. In that case, I might have to smack him upside the head."

Instead, my reply to his "love questions" e-mail was simple. "*Non. Non, merci. Bonne chance à vous.*"

Finally, his e-mails stopped. Maybe he just didn't understand, "No," in English.

A Handful of Mixed Nuts

I will start this installment with a retired bachelor, at the upper end of my range age. His profile picture screamed Hannibal Lecter, sans straight jacket.

His introductory e-mail read: "I had a dream about you last night. I couldn't stop kissing your neck. I think it was the musk oil and your soft skin creating a sweet spot I couldn't resist! Do you think that is a typical guy thought, or is it possible that women really are special to me? Just wondering… CyberCasanova."

What the ???

Typical guys do not think this way. Musk oil? Who talks about, much less dreams about, musk oil? As far as being special goes, maybe the kind of "special" that is tonight's dinner entrée with fava beans and Chianti.

I don't know about you, but that was entirely too bizarre for me. There was no, "Hello," or even a, "Good evening." I can not believe this guy thought that was an acceptable introductory greeting.

I replied, "Honestly, I found it to be forward and creepy since we don't know each other. I wish you luck finding a match."

"I think you misinterpreted my comedic style e-mail about a thought experiment of how men think when we see a pretty girl and react with romance laden thoughts of love and affection as if we fast forwarded through courting to a point in the relationship where friendship develops into partners."

Huh? A comedic thought experiment? I didn't find any of it particularly funny. It has been said that there is a fine line between genius and insanity. This guy seemed to have crossed that line.

"It didn't come across as comedic. You might want to rethink your approach. Best of luck to you."

He replied, "We are what our genes say we are and if it's a smiling, happy, pretty girl that lifts us to happiness to want to live another day, then the Cosmos has set forth profound physical laws and properties to help ensure the survival of our species. A gentleman knows to look but not touch unless given permission. The Devil doesn't make us, the Cosmos does. You're probably just another fake profiler that doesn't know the difference between E=mc2 and their hat size. Just sayin'… CyberEinstein."

You're freaking nuts! And obviously, the Cosmos is slacking big time, because you've survived this long.

I loved his slams on my integrity and intelligence. I think I will refer to him as "CyberNutJob." And the Cosmos did not make me say it, nor did the Devil. I did it all on my own without consulting my genetic code or altering the space-time continuum.

The next man did not want to take, "No," for an answer. He was within my age range. However, we had nothing in common based on our profiles. Absolutely positively nothing.

Every picture posted was shirtless. Most were old pictures. They looked like Polaroids from the 1970s. His profile and e-mails were written in all capital letters. So, he was lazy on top of everything else.

I apologize for the caps, but I wanted to give you the true essence of the exchange.

"JULIET...LET ME BE YOUR ROMEO."

"We do not have enough in common. I wish you luck finding a match."

"ROMEO NEEDS YOU...I'LL COME TO YOU....I PROMISE I'M AS GOOD AS ADVERTISED...ONLY 10 TIMES BETTER!"

"No, thank you."

"ROMEO CAN'T BE ROMEO WITHOUT YOU."

I did not reply.

Two days later, he sent, "I KNOW...YOU SAID NO...I DO RESPECT THAT...BUT I TRULY BELIEVE YOU MISSED JUDGED ME."

No, I definitely did not. All I want to do is correct your grammar, spelling, and punctuation.

I answered, "You do not respect me because you keep contacting me. My answer is no."

"I DO RESPECT...BUT COULD YOU TELL ME WHY...MAYBE I'LL LEARN SOMETHING. BE NICE."

Oh my God! Seriously? Okay, buddy, you asked for it. And I'll try to be as nice as possible.

Annoyed, I typed, "No, you really don't respect me because you insist on making me justify my answer. You are not my type, and I am not attracted to you. You have cats. You smoke. You want children. You have so many grammatical errors in your profile, I lost track. You indicate that you will become violent when defending loved ones. You posted shirtless pictures only. And last, but not least, you refuse to take, 'No,' for an answer. Nothing you say will cause me to change my mind. Please do not contact me again."

Well, you know he did. I ignored him, and he eventually went away.

The next unsuccessful candidate was a retired lawyer. He was well out of my age range.

He wrote, "Good looking, sometimes charming, generally well-behaved lawyer calling."

"You have a dog, and I am severely allergic to dogs. I wish you luck finding a match."

Pleading his case, he replied, "Pity. Outside of my dog we are a pretty good romantic prospect. I'm as pretty as you, and as smart, creative, sophisticated, and wealthy as you'll find in these parts. Don't rule me out on the onset."

Friends, he was not as pretty as me. Not even close. God forgive me, but the way he styled his red hair made him look like a clown. Not Stephen King's, *It*, clown, more like a circus clown.

"My reaction to animals is anaphylactic. So I can not be around them or people who own them. Best of luck."

He persisted, "I have a solution! No hugging, kissing, or ETC. pending the occurrence of at least one of the following:

1) You become uncontrollably driven to hug, kiss, or etc. with me so as to suffer a bad reaction notwithstanding.

In your freaking dreams!

2) You become gradually (and miraculously) acclimated. (I GROW ON YOU)

You would grow on me like a flesh-eating disease!

3) You take a Sudafed or other effective medication. (I will pay for testing and treatment- ha ha)

Over-the-counter meds don't work for anaphylaxis, moron.

4) I take a ridiculously thorough bath beforehand. (You can watch!)

Yuck!!! I shudder at the mere thought. You could not pay me to watch.

5) My poor dog dies.

I pity that dog for having to put up with you.

6) We give it a CAREFUL AND JUDICIOUS TRY.

Oh sure, because you're not the one risking your life. Easy for you to say, "Let's give it a shot." You're not the one who could die.

"Let's meet for coffee, sweetness, I promise you won't get the hives!"

Not if you were the last man on earth!

Life with this guy would consist of one idiotic, never-ending argument after another. Talk about exhausting.

In my closing argument, I responded, "I am not persuaded by your arguments. Anaphylaxis is not like a regular allergy. There is no medication I can take to avoid it. I am sorry, but my answer is still no. I wish you luck finding a match."

Still refusing to acknowledge my lack of interest, he replied, "I know perfectly well the effects of anaphylactic shock. It is after all, an allergic reaction, which is not unique to yourself. Changes in your physical environment could ameliorate the symptoms. In addition to physical factors, the power of the mind cannot be ignored and can produce remarkable things."

Sure! Let me just mentally will my throat not to close and miraculously stop myself from dying due to the lack of oxygen. Gee, why didn't I think of that before? If it was that easy, I would have tried it with the cowboy from a few articles back. I would not waste my newly-discovered superpowers on the likes of you.

I did not reply because I knew he would keep arguing. He sent four more e-mails. I ignored each one.

Then, a short time later, he sent the same initial e-mail to me. Another quickly followed. It read, "Oops forgot! You're the anti-dog screwball, never mind."

As I shook my head in dismay, a little voice beckoned to me. Behold! It is a jar of Nutella calling my name.

Mmm ... hazelnuts. The kind of nuts a girl can truly love!

It Finally Happened!

It finally happened! About two weeks ago, I received the most unbelievable message from the online dating site. It was short and to the point. I read it twice before it sank in. I just could not believe my eyes. But there it was staring me in the face. It read, "0 Matches Found."

Yes, I accomplished the seemingly impossible feat. I exhausted all of my possible matches on this website. Even with my extended search range of 100 miles and age range of 35 to 55, there were no matches. None. Nada. Zip. Zilch.

I hear you saying, "Well, you're being too picky."

No, I'm not. I'm giving a 20-year age range within 100 miles. All hair and eye colors, all body types, except obese, all religions, and a college degree.

My primary problem is that almost everybody in this state has indoor pets. Over half of my supposed matches were eliminated due to a pet situation.

Granted, some guys say they will get rid of their pets. But I still couldn't go into their houses or ride in their cars. They would have to rip out the carpets, replace their furniture, clean the house's ductwork, etc. Not many men would go through that or have the financial means to do so.

Not to be deterred, I thought I should try another dating service. So, I signed up on a Christian website. Their questions were quite different than those found on the other dating service's website.

Would you engage in premarital sex?
Is my mom running this site?
Do you believe that the only reason to engage in sexual relations is for procreation?
Um, no.
How often ideally would you want to have sexual relations? The answers ranged from "every day" to "never."
I plead the Fifth on my answer to this question.
I am sensing an anti-sex theme here. Seriously? Never? If you want to remain eternally celibate, you should look into becoming a Catholic nun or a priest. They need new recruits.

I particularly loved the questions that revolved around my children, especially since I don't have any. There was no way to bypass the questions. So, I had to base my answers on the imaginary children that I don't have and never will have.

Other questions asked about the woman's role in the home. Those questions pissed me off. It upset me to think that there are women who are acting subservient to men. That's an entire blog post, in and of itself.

I found one useful question: How is your timeliness?
I am always early. If you are habitually late, then you will be literally and figuratively wasting my time. Do us both a favor, do not waste my time.
There were so many absurd questions, I wish I could share them

all. But one of my favorites was: How do you feel about wearing fashionable clothes?

Oh, just throw a burlap sack over my head, and I'll tie it around my waist with some twine, thank you. Itchy is all the rage this season!

The more questions I answered, the more I felt I was falling down the rabbit hole, and I was positive I would end up in Wonderland. Remember, Wonderland was royally screwed up.

After suffering through the questions and filling out the profile, their system told me I had zero matches. I laughed out loud. No kidding. So, I went to the search feature and altered some criteria. Ten guys popped up. I recognized six of them from the previous website. The others had no pictures. I do not communicate with men who do not post pictures.

After five days on this site, I wanted to shoot myself. I searched to cover anyone breathing and with a pulse within 100 miles. There was not one single soul remotely close to what I was looking for in a partner. The majority of profiles had no pictures, and the men lived in rural areas, and very few had graduated from college.

The system sent me profiles to view. Most of the men lived in Illinois or Ohio.

I was done. So, I called to cancel. The best the girl could do was downgrade my account to one month instead of the original six. *Wonderful.*

Obviously, some people have found that site successful. I am happy for them. Sorry to say that I was not one of them.

Since that went so poorly, I joined yet another dating site. I had no matches on that site either. But this service didn't allow me to search for matches. I had to wait until they decided to send me someone.

Really, there was no way to search. Instead, I kept answering questions. I answered 290 questions. Yes, I answered that many. I was just sitting on my couch watching television on a Saturday night, so why not?

I got messages saying, "So-and-so is just outside of your parameters."

The majority of men were from other states. Not neighboring states like Illinois or Ohio, but states such as Texas, New Jersey, Florida, and California.

The ones that really astonished me were the matches who were technically incompatible based on our answers. If we answered 67% of the questions differently, in my mind, we were not a match. But those were the profiles the computer kept sending me.

This service was the most expensive. So, I wrote their Customer Service people a nasty-gram.

"You only send me 'matches' who are outside of my parameters. What is the point of answering all of the questions if you ignore them when matching people? I'm getting 'matches' when over 50% of our answers differ. Those aren't matches.

And I am not interested in anyone who lives out of state. You repeatedly send me guys who live all over the country. How can I get you to stop sending me people who live out of state? It's ridiculous. I'm not looking for a pen pal. I'm looking for a mate.

So far, this service has been a waste of time and money. What are you going to do to make this a better experience for me?"

And I waited. I was not sure what type of response I expected. I just wanted to notify them that their computer algorithms sucked, and I was unhappy. Less than twelve hours later, I received a response.

"Our goal is to find matches for you that are compatible with your unique personality in deep and important ways. We do this by using the results of your relationship questionnaire to screen for individuals based on the 29 Dimensions of Compatibility.

We understand that you won't feel a connection with all of your matches. Although we put a lot of emphasis here in the early stages of being matched with someone, establishing chemistry only accounts for a portion of what makes a relationship last and is only something you can determine once you get to know someone. We caution you from trying to make such an early assessment from just the match detail information. Please be assured that you will no longer receive matches outside your distance setting."

I wished I had a pair of hip waders to trudge through that pile of BS.

Just when I thought all hope was lost, I received an e-mail from the first dating service I tried. There was a considerable influx of new members. Summer was over. All of the kids were back to school, and dads were back into dating mode. So, I returned to browse the offerings on that site.

Faithful readers, I know you enjoy these stories, but nothing would make me happier than to have a reason to stop writing them. Wish me luck!

Fright or Delight?

My quest to find a good, decent man is becoming epic in length. I refuse to give up! Being a poet at heart, I wrote this poem about the next group of non-matches.

There once was a man who was prolific in poem and prose.
He had a quick wit. Let's meet. Why not? Who knows?
Alas, his memory was lacking, he called me by the wrong name,
Despite me correcting him over and over. How totally lame.
Was this other woman his ex-girlfriend or an ex-wife?
I cared not, for I was cutting him out of my life.

The next eager bachelor was an eHarmonious man
Who unfortunately decided to try a product to self-tan.
Since he was not an Oompa Loompa, orange was an awful hue.
Why he did not realize this while looking in the mirror, I have no freaking clue.
However, it was his obnoxious behavior that upset me the most.
Being rude and insensitive caused him to end up as a jerk in this post.

Then there was a guy who promised me a special surprise.

When the big reveal occurred, I could hardly believe my eyes.
If I was watching a horror movie, I would have yelled for the girl to run.
Touring ramshackle buildings buried deep in the woods was not my idea of fun.
Any chemistry that might have existed was extinguished pretty fast.
What a huge letdown after being psyched up for an absolute blast.

After each date, to Mom, the obligatory e-mail I did write,
So she wouldn't be pacing the floor half of the night,
Worried that I was dead in a ditch or suffering an even worse fate.
"Home safe and sound." Another zero of a date.
"A total waste of makeup," was what I eventually would type.
It summed up the evenings well, without painfully boring details or hype.

So that, gentle readers, is all I have to tell.
Perhaps the month of October will cast an enchanting spell.
Could the eclipse of the blood moon help me find my "Mr. Right?"
Or will it bring more ghouls and goblins to give me an awful fright?
Those are the questions that I seek the answers for.
Stay tuned, my friends, you never know what's in store!

The Twelve Days of Christmas

Christmas Greetings! My online dating adventures inspired me to write a satirical tune for the season. Some material writes itself!

On the first day of Christmas, Match did give to me,
A bachelor with a dog that has fleas.

On the second day of Christmas, Match did give to me,
Two heavy drinkers,
And a bachelor with a dog that has fleas.

On the third day of Christmas, Match did give to me,
Three not so wise men,
Two heavy drinkers,
And a bachelor with a dog that has fleas.

On the fourth day of Christmas, Match did give to me,
Four scary stalkers,
Three not so wise men,
Two heavy drinkers,
And a bachelor with a dog that has fleas.

On the fifth day of Christmas, Match did give to me,
Five narcissistic cads,
Four scary stalkers,
Three not so wise men,
Two heavy drinkers,
And a bachelor with a dog that has fleas.

On the sixth day of Christmas, Match did give to me,
Six months for free,
Five narcissistic cads,
Four scary stalkers,
Three not so wise men,
Two heavy drinkers,
And a bachelor with a dog that has fleas.

On the seventh day of Christmas, Match did give to me,
Seven guys my dad's age,
Six months for free,
Five narcissistic cads,
Four scary stalkers,
Three not so wise men,
Two heavy drinkers,
And a bachelor with a dog that has fleas.

On the eighth day of Christmas, Match did give to me,
Eight lewd propositions,
Seven dudes my dad's age,
Six months for free,
Five narcissistic cads,
Four scary stalkers,
Three not so wise men,

Two heavy drinkers,
And a bachelor with a dog that has fleas.

On the ninth day of Christmas, Match did give to me,
Nine fancy dinners,
Eight lewd propositions,
Seven dudes my dad's age,
Six months for free,
Five narcissistic cads,
Four scary stalkers,
Three not so wise men,
Two heavy drinkers,
And a bachelor with a dog that has fleas.

On the tenth day of Christmas, Match did give to me,
Ten hotties under thirty,
Nine fancy dinners,
Eight lewd propositions,
Seven dudes my dad's age,
Six months for free,
Five narcissistic cads,
Four scary stalkers,
Three not so wise men,
Two heavy drinkers,
And a bachelor with a dog that has fleas.

On the eleventh day of Christmas, Match did give to me,
Eleven filthy pictures,
Ten hotties under thirty,
Nine fancy dinners,
Eight lewd propositions,

Seven dudes my dad's age,
Six months for free,
Five narcissistic cads,
Four scary stalkers,
Three not so wise men,
Two heavy drinkers,
And a bachelor with a dog that has fleas.

On the twelfth day of Christmas, Match did give to me,
Twelve illiterate bumpkins,
Eleven filthy pictures,
Ten hotties under thirty,
Nine fancy dinners,
Eight lewd propositions,
Seven dudes my dad's age,
Six months for free,
Five narcissistic cads,
Four scary stalkers,
Three not so wise men,
Two heavy drinkers,
And a bachelor with a dog that has fleas!

Just Say, "No!"

According to online dating statistics, January 4th is the biggest sign-up day for their sites. That gave me a new glimmer of hope. Although, so far, Indianapolis' bachelors seemed to be singing the same old song—same tune, just different words.

The initial contact e-mail from one guy read, "My view of your profile indicates we are a 97% match. If we were any more alike, you would have strong biceps and I would have boobs."

I had to assume he thought I would find that funny. He guessed wrong. I could not find words to reply. I take that back. I did have words. I just didn't want to engage him in conversation. Any guy that tacky in an introductory e-mail did not deserve a reply.

A retired sales executive, who was out of my desired age range, contacted me. He did not have pets and thought we were a perfect match. His profile indicated he was a cigar aficionado and ultimate sun worshiper. So, I had my doubts.

Among other questions, I inquired, "How often do you smoke?"

He replied, "I don't smoke. Well, occasionally, a stogie and of course pot."

Of course pot?

This is not Colorado or Amsterdam, the last time I checked. This man was in his late 50s. He was not some punk kid or Olympian gold medalist, Michael Phelps.

I responded, "I don't do drugs and will not date anyone who does. If getting high is part of your life, then this is where our conversation ends."

I never heard from him again.

The next bachelor's e-mail claimed he was a gemologist from New York City, and that his business takes him all over the world.

Not interested, I replied, "You live over 700 miles away. So I'm not sure why you're looking in Indiana. Logistically, it doesn't make any sense. I'm not looking for a long distance relationship."

"If I find the right woman, I shall relocate to be closer to her or even live in the same house with her."

Oh, I bet you would like living off of a woman, wouldn't you?

"No. Best of luck to you."

Later, I received another e-mail. "It will interest you to know that I have been thinking of you all day and I really want this to work between us and as of the distance that shouldn't be a problem because like I said earlier that I shall be relocating closer to you. All what I need now to bail myself out of financial struggle is just 25,000 dollars and I have 21,000 already what I need is 4000 can you help me YES or NO no long mails and explanation."

"NO!"

Wow! It was bad enough that he was trying to swindle me out of money, but to demand an answer immediately, with no explanation, that was ridiculous. Apparently, he was an impatient thief and did not want to waste time if he wasn't going to get a payoff. I assumed I would not hear from this scammer again. No such luck.

The following day, he wrote again. "Why the silent? A friend in salt lake want to transfer me money into account but I can not access my account here so I was thinking if they can transfer the money into your account when you get it, you will send it to me using western union the amount is about 5000 or 6000 can you help me? I need money urgently here in Turkey to get out of here."

Turkey can have you!

The fatal flaw in this scammer's logic was that the friend could send the money via Western Union. I think it was a foreign ring of thieves. The English in the initial communication was acceptable. However, it went downhill with each subsequent exchange. Who knows?

It worried me that some people might be gullible enough to fall for this scam. I reported him, but his profile and any trace of him were gone.

Beware of low-life scammers! They are everywhere!

After talking for the good part of a week, I dined with a project manager from the south side of Indianapolis. I liked that he preferred talking to texting. I found that encouraging. When we met, I realized he was a little bit country, and I was a little bit rock and roll. He seemed uncomfortable and out of his element at the restaurant. I hemmed and hawed about whether to go on another date with him.

The following day, I received a text from an unknown number.

"Why the f*** do you have my f***ing number saved? Get out of here and leave me and him's relationship ALONE. Bye now."

It was followed by an emoticon of an expressive hand. Use your imagination.

Huh? Nice mouth! And me and him's?

I felt bad for the poor, functionally illiterate woman with the cheating boyfriend. Believing it was a wrong number, I replied, "I have no idea who you are or who you're talking about. I think you have the wrong number."

No response.

About an hour later, I got a call from the guy. "I'm sorry, but I'm not over my ex. Just wanted to let you know. I'm gonna take myself off this site. I shouldn't date until I'm over her. Sorry."

Are you kidding me?

Maybe it wasn't a wrong number after all. I could not believe it. The more I thought about it, I became more ticked off. He used me to make his ex jealous. Wow! That was a new low.

The next candidate also liked talking on the phone. We met at a café. He appeared nervous and claimed he had butterflies in his stomach about meeting me or possibly it was a lactose intolerance problem. Okay, no big deal.

About an hour into our conversation, which was pretty one-sided, he departed for the bathroom. Upon returning, he announced he was really sick, the I-need-to-spend-the-day-in-the-bathroom kind of sick. He confessed he had been ill since the previous day.

I wished him well, literally, and we parted ways.

What kind of person shows up sick to a first date? It was a complete and utter lack of respect and common courtesy.

People, if you are sick, stay home and reschedule!

He contacted me days later to say that he did not remember anything about our date or what we discussed. He said he remembered he liked me and my cleavage, but that was all. He wanted another date.

Um, no. My cleavage and I think not.

I have no rational explanation for why the men in this area are so relationship-challenged. If anyone has a theory, then I'm all ears. Better yet, if you know of a decent single guy, send him my way. The Law of Averages dictates there has to be some decent guys out there somewhere!

Could Business Lead to Pleasure?

I found it interesting that many of my former coworkers were popping up in my search results. I told myself I would not date someone I used to work with because of the ugly rumor mill. However, since my options were pretty sparse, I made a few exceptions.

There was one sweet, caring, and nurturing guy who took care of me after I had an accident. He checked on me before he went to work and again on his way home from work. He picked up my prescriptions, went grocery shopping for me, and when I felt well enough, he took me out to dinner. I even went to church with him a few times. This went on for weeks. Then I made an honest mistake. After we had hugged for the umpteenth time, I kissed him.

He could not leave my house fast enough. Usually, I had the opposite problem. Sometimes I needed a crowbar or a large stick to get a man off of me. His reaction was completely unexpected.

The next time we spoke, he explained, "Kissing leads to other things."

Dude, I kissed you. I didn't rip off your clothes and jump you.

He suggested that I watch some videos that his church posted online.

I watched. The gist of the videos was that you should not have any physical or romantic contact with the person you're dating. I found it unsettling. Withholding affection is abnormal and controlling behavior. I consider it to be mental and emotional abuse. And I told him so.

To make a long story short, dating was not an option. However, we remained friends. He eventually got over the no-physical-contact and no-kissing things. He has since married.

I remember the time I met the next guy at work about twenty years ago. There was something about him that made me stop and take notice. I was married at the time. So, that's where the story ended. That is, until I saw him online.

I contacted him, and we went on some dates. I was still attracted to him. But he smoked, and we didn't have common interests.

A short time after our last date, I was grocery shopping with my mother. As we rounded a corner, he and his daughter appeared. I introduced him to my mother. He introduced us to his daughter. She was adorable. During the course of the conversation, he said some slightly odd things. His precocious daughter felt the need to correct him. After exchanging a few more pleasantries, we went our separate ways.

Mom turned to me. "You dated that one, didn't you?"

I laughed. "Yeah. How'd you know?"

"The poor guy was tongue-tied, and his daughter kept looking at him like he'd lost his mind. It was funny. Are you still seeing him?"

"No. He's a nice guy. I used to work with him. We don't have a lot in common."

"That's too bad. He was good-looking, and his daughter was a riot."

A handful of my former coworkers who received my e-mail updates sent me contact information for their siblings, cousins, next door neighbors, and friends. None of those worked out. Many thanks to all who tried though. I appreciated your efforts.

Dysfunctional Dates Abound

Polite social interaction appears to be going the way of the dodo bird. Where is Miss Manners when I need her?

A 54-year-old IT professional passed the e-mail test but failed the phone conversation test miserably. During the course of the conversation, he brought up the subject of sex.

He clearly stated his view on the subject, and I quote, "By the third date, a woman should be ready to give up the goods."

Where do I start with this? Even if this guy bought me three very expensive dinners at St. Elmo's, I would not consider that appropriate criteria to have sex.

And goods?

I was sure he would have wanted the entire package of "goods and services." Honestly, in the sex department, the goods aren't quite as enjoyable without the accompanying services.

Nevertheless, this girl and her "goods and services" are worth a lot more than three dinners, even if decadent desserts are included!

Next was a 52-year-old executive at a large company in

Indianapolis. He successfully navigated the phone interview, but live, he was a completely different person.

I have nicknamed him, "The Negative Bachelor." The restaurant was too warm. The fire made the air too dry. He asked the waiter questions about the precise origin of the seafood. The poor kid had no idea.

Dude, if you want the salmon, order the freaking salmon.

Then he substituted the sides, not due to an allergy or health reason, but because, "The chef obviously doesn't know how to pair sides with entrées."

When the food arrived, he complained that his potatoes were too lumpy. The carrots were too soft, the squash was too hard. His chardonnay was not as good as the chardonnay he had last week.

My mahi-mahi, wherever it was from, was fantastic. I loved my lumpy mashed potatoes and steamed vegetables.

To my surprise, he insisted on ordering dessert. Why? I don't know. He did not enjoy the rest of the meal. Why he wanted to perpetuate the experience was beyond me. He ordered cheesecake.

Guess how that turned out.

It was not as good as the cheesecake he had had in New York City the previous month.

I gazed into the fire, which under different circumstances might have been romantic, and attempted to drown myself in the chocolate dessert I ordered. It was delicious. I scraped my plate to savor every drop of chocolatey goodness. Alas, not even the chocolate could make up for the bad company.

As a change of pace, a well-intentioned friend set me up on a blind date with a guy she knew. He was my age, and he looked okay in a picture she showed me.

He walked into the restaurant wearing a baseball hat, chomping on a piece of gum. The hat never left his head. The gum chewing was distracting, to say the least. Finally, he took the gum out of his mouth. My praise to God was short-lived.

There are a multitude of things you can do to dispose of chewed gum. You could dispose of it prior to meeting your date for the first time. Or, you could excuse yourself to the men's room and throw it away in there. Or, you could dispose of it in a napkin.

Did he do any of those things? Unfortunately, no.

Instead, he removed the gum from his mouth and stuck it on the side of his drinking glass. Then, he proceeded to play with the gum like it was Silly Putty. When he finished eating, wait for it—he put that same piece of gum back into his mouth.

I can only imagine that the look on my face mirrored the utter and complete dismay and disgust I felt. Too bad no one took a picture of me. It would have brilliantly captured that Kodak moment for sure.

Moving on to a seemingly, happy-go-lucky guy, 50 years of age. He readily admitted that his mood was due to his habitual pot usage.

I flatly stated, "I don't do drugs, and I don't want to be around anyone who does."

"I've been doing it for as long as I remember. But for you, I'd give it up."

Uh huh. "Sure."

Then with his next breath, he said, "You should try it though. You'll like it. It will make you more creative."

I refused, "No. I have no desire to. Never have, never will. I'm creative enough."

He argued, "It will make you more creative than you ever

imagined. You don't know what you're missing. All the great artists do it."

I disagreed, "I'm not missing anything."

Out of left field, he said, "You know, sex is only good if you get high beforehand."

"Wow! If you have to get high to enjoy sex, you're not doing it right."

So far this year, there has been a plethora of overbearing, controlling bachelors. All of the men were in their fifties. Yeah, I was on an older guy run for some time. I ran out of forty-somethings without any pets. I am not sure if the over-fifty statistic has anything to do with it, or if it was just coincidence.

The common theme was men telling me all of the things that I should and/or need to do. Here are a few, in no particular order.

"You need to learn to play golf."

"I'm not really interested in golf. I have other interests. It's great that you play golf with your college buddies so often."

"You need to learn. I play golf, so you need to play."

"We have different interests. We don't have to do everything together."

"Yes, we do."

Thinking he was joking, I laughed and responded, "No, we don't. But I could drive the golf cart."

Sternly and slowly, he said, "You're not hearing me."

Oh yes, I am, Mr. Control Freak. Yikes!

"You should join my gym. It's the best one in the city."

"I exercise at home."

"That's not good enough. You need to join the gym, so you can get buff."

"I'm happy with my body the way it is."

"You have areas of your body that need improvement."

Excuse me?

I will be the first one to admit my body is not perfect. But I do not need a man telling me that my body needs improvement on a first date.

"You should wear higher heels."

"I'm comfortable in these."

"I like higher heels."

Then you wear them. "These are the highest ones I have."

"You need to buy higher ones. You'd look sexier."

I laughed. "Trust me, I wouldn't. I am not graceful in four-inch heels."

Looking at me very intensely, he whispered, "Babe, your feet would never touch the floor. Ever."

Not exactly appropriate first date conversation. And I hate being called, "Babe."

"I want to throw you on the back of my Harley and head down to Brown County."

"Brown County is beautiful, but I don't ride motorcycles."

"You just need to try it."

"Already tried it. I rode on one once. I didn't like it at all. I won't do it again."

"I'll change your mind. Guaranteed."

"Sorry, you won't. I like road trips in a car. Those are fun—rain or shine."

"You're just a stuck-up bitch, aren't you?"
Heavy sigh.

These exchanges are just a sampling of what I deal with daily. Time and time again, polite conversation is nowhere to be found. Men continually attempt to pressure me to do something I am not interested in doing.

Why do these men feel as if they have to force women to do or like everything they do? I am sure Dr. Phil has done plenty of shows on this subject. But it still baffles me.

I do not try to force my interests and hobbies on anyone. I would never dream of it. We are all individuals. We do not have to be identical on everything.

Potential mates should have similar mindsets. That way, we can appreciate each other's likes and dislikes to discover things to do together as a couple.

The problem with online dating algorithms is that they can not analyze mindsets. Hence, my ongoing conundrum.

My Big, Fat Greek Tragedy

If there was any doubt that my life is a Greek tragedy in the making, this story should solidify the notion in everyone's minds.

This suitor was a well-known businessman, in his early 50s. When he contacted me, I turned him down. One of the descriptors in his profile did not sit right with me. I explained in my reply that descriptor was why I turned him down.

He wrote me a long e-mail in return, clarifying his position and dispelling any incorrect impressions. His arguments were good ones. I agreed to talk to him.

We talked and decided to meet. However, he was in Florida vacationing with his kids. Our date would have to wait until he returned. Despite that he was vacationing, we spoke every day.

Then, my dad had a heart attack. I drove to New York as this intriguing man drove back to Indiana.

God just loves messing with me.

The guy understood, and we kept chatting on the phone.

Finally, we were in the same city at the same time. After talking for almost three weeks, we met for dinner. We got along splendidly. Our likes and dislikes were the same in just about all areas, including politics and religion.

He grew up on the East Coast, just like me. Loved to travel. Loved live theater and musicals! Yes, musicals! Where had he been hiding all of this time?

Well, most of the time, he was working, networking, or attending his kids' activities. He had the busiest calendar I had ever seen. He could not plan out more than a week ahead because meetings and events were constantly being added to his schedule by his assistant and his kids. He swore he would make time for me. And he did try.

In the days that followed, we talked for hours on end, about everything and anything. The conversation never got stale or boring. The more we got to know one another, the more perfect we seemed for each other. The similarities were uncanny.

Drinking and smoking were not issues. *Awesome!*

His children were older. *Another bonus.*

He had no pets and had no intention of ever owning one. *Thank you, Jesus! Pinch me already!*

Anyway, everything was going pretty well until it was time to meet his friends. That's when the bottom dropped out.

While Mr. Seemingly-Perfect did not have any pets, every single one of his friends did. These friends were his work colleagues as well as his personal friends. He spent almost all of his time with these people.

The dilemma was that they all entertained in their houses. You know, where the animals lived. Extended exposure to these animals would literally kill me.

Meeting his friends out at a restaurant would have been fine. I suggested that. But in the long run, that would not have been feasible or sustainable, as they all loved to entertain at their homes. Each had an elaborate backyard oasis, fire pit, and/or boat, etc.

Then there was his buddy's lake house. I absolutely love lake houses. I love sitting by a lake, looking out at the water, and listening to the water lap up on the shore. There's nothing quite like watching the sun rise or set over the water.

That's one of the biggest things I miss about living in New York. I really miss being close to a large body of water. Growing up minutes from Lake Ontario was a luxury I did not fully appreciate until I moved to Indiana, land of small, man-made lakes. But I digress …

There were always animals at his buddy's lake house. The owner brought his pets and allowed everyone to bring their pets too. Well, just shoot me now, and put me out of my misery.

I could not in good conscience ask him to pick between me and his friends. He's known some of them for over twenty years. If I kept him from them, he would become resentful. And I would feel guilty.

If he always went over to his friends' houses and to the lake house without me, I would become resentful. And presumably, he would feel guilty.

We discussed the situation rationally. No compromise was suitable. He picked his friends.

I won't lie. I was extremely disappointed. However, the reality was that I could never compete with them, the lifestyle to which he had grown accustomed, the boats, and the lake house.

Talk about pitiful. We couldn't have a relationship because of other people's pets.

Heavy sigh.

Animals are truly the bane of my existence.

Awkward Moments

My life has become a series of awkward moments. I've interacted with enough men that sooner or later, I run into them. Sometimes the accidental meetings are cordial. Other times, I want to crawl under a table or run the other way.

The first time this happened was at a poetry reading. My poems were about a specific man I had dated. If you were wondering, he broke up with me. He showed up to the reading with a girlfriend on his arm. He even introduced her to me. I hadn't dated anyone since our breakup. And I had attended the event alone.

The show must go on! So, I recited my love poems, in front of the man who inspired them, while he held his new girlfriend's hand.

While on Facebook one day, I received a friend request from a one-date guy. We had not friended each other prior to, or after, our one date, over a year ago. I found the request to be odd. I clicked on the request and saw that he had gotten married.

I did not accept the request. I messaged him, "I'm sure you don't want to be friends. I'm guessing that you wanted me to see that you are married and you moved. I am happy for you, and I'm glad you're doing well. I wish you the best."

He responded, "Either that, or it was because your picture popped up as 'is this someone you know?' Forgive and forget, two things I love about freedom from cynicism. Hope you are well and writing lots of interesting blogs these days!"

Fine, call me a cynic. But I wasn't born yesterday. He follows my author page and knows I'm still single. He wanted to make sure I knew that he was happily married.

The next encounter occurred while I was waiting for a friend in the lobby of a movie theater. This guy was one of my one-date guys. He was in line with his kids. He recognized me. We exchanged pleasantries before they moved on to watch their movie. If only all of my accidental meetings went that well.

I was having dinner with a two-date guy when a former four-date guy was seated at the table next to us, facing me. If looks could have killed, you wouldn't be reading this book. After our initial eye-contact, I refused to look at him. But I felt his glare throughout the meal. He even said some insulting things loudly, to upset me. I opted out of dessert just to escape.

I have had numerous run-ins at grocery stores and restaurants. In general, if the man is with a woman, he will acknowledge me in some form or another. It's probably an ego thing for them. But I'm happy that they found someone more suitable than me. The single guys, on the other hand, are a mixed bag. They usually ignore me. However, if I broke up with the guy, I might get a death stare or even a drunken text later that night.

Talking to guys I discarded, for one reason or another, isn't on my "To Do" List anyway. Every once and awhile, I receive an e-mail or text from an old boyfriend. Most are on a fishing expedition to see if they can get another chance. Sorry, but I'm a catch-and-release girl. If I let you go, then I'm done with you. That makes you fair game for the other women trolling in the sea.

I went out to dinner with a friend, who had just broken up with his girlfriend. He asked me to tell him one of my dating disaster stories to cheer him up. I decided to tell him the crossdresser story, in its entirety. He enjoyed my misfortune and laughed heartily.

About ten minutes later, a couple stopped at our table.

The man greeted me, "Hi, Suzanne. Great to see you. Hope you two have a nice evening."

Surprised, I answered, "Hi! Great to see you. Hope you do too."

They walked away and out of the restaurant.

Frantic, I asked my friend, "Were they behind us?"

He replied, "I don't know. I wasn't paying attention."

I pressed, "Think! Where were they sitting?"

Nonchalantly, he said, "I really couldn't tell you."

"Oh shit! I hope they weren't behind us."

Confused, he asked, "What's the big deal?"

Sighing, I admitted, "That was the crossdresser."

My friend burst into hysterical laughter.

I wanted to die.

Mind you, I didn't say anything mean or untrue. I just relayed the story of this nice, handsome guy who happened to be a crossdresser. But I still wanted to die.

To this day, I don't know where they sat or if they overheard me.

It's Hard to Be Arm Candy

This tale of woe involves a man about whom you have already read. I believed he was worth a second chance. However, that chance was short-lived.

In life, timing is everything. He admitted his schedule was not conducive to dating. That was a gross understatement. And so, he broke my already-wounded heart. This article is more about my experience at this party than about him though.

I never revealed to him how I felt. As the saying goes, if you don't have something nice to say, then don't say anything at all. But, hell, as a blogger and author, I have to write something!

We attended a large social function together. The food was fantastic, and the live band was really good.

As the event progressed, everyone seemed to be having a wonderful time. Everyone except for me, that is.

The event was industry-specific. Truthfully, it was a field in which I had little interest. Normally, I would make small talk. That's easy enough to do, right? People are people. Lord knows I can talk about anything. However, the other attendees were not into small talk. They were laser-focused on their field.

When I was introduced to people, they seemed disinterested, since

I was not part of their "inner circle." The only question I received from a few of them was, "Do you have any children?" When I answered, "No," that was the end of the conversation. I was flabbergasted. End of conversation. They turned to engage someone else in a discussion. Time is money. Money is time.

What planet am I on that the only question anyone wants to ask me is that one? I have no children. Ergo, I am not worth talking to.

I have a lot to offer, thank you, very much. I have plenty to say and have a slew of great stories, just ask me something else. Anything else!

I felt as if I had developed a superpower instantaneously—I became totally invisible! Since I did not add any perceived value, I was not worth their time.

Mind you, I had an opinion of what they were discussing, but since I was not a player, my opinion would not have mattered. So, I kept my mouth shut. Picture that if you can.

For some time, I smiled and paid attention to the discussion. However, as time wore on, I surrendered. I allowed my mind to wander as I smiled and nodded at what seemed appropriate times.

I watched a child torment a bug in the grass. I saw an older man nod off, only to have his wife poke him and wake him up. I watched one of the waiters fill cups of lemonade and iced tea and line them up on a table. He dutifully replaced them when a guest would walk off with one. There were twenty-one cups. I wondered why he did not choose an even number.

I spotted a trail that went off into a wooded area. I desperately wanted to slip away and explore where the path led. But I decided that would be in bad form. Instead, I remained glued to my seat.

Then, I counted the tent poles and estimated the tent to be approximately 1300 ft x 40 ft. I did not hazard a guess on height because of the varying heights from the edges to the center. If I had a pen and paper, I might have been able to figure it out mathematically. *Not.* I was not *that* bored!

In all of my forty-six years, this was the first time I have ever been excluded to the point that I felt like arm candy.

Good Lord, being arm candy was a tough job! I had no idea! And I didn't even suffer through a boob job, tanning sessions, liposuction, or Botox injections.

As a child, my parents always told me I could do anything. Well, I learned in first grade that I would never be a gymnast or an athlete of any kind. Obviously, over the years, I discovered other things I could not or would not do. Being arm candy just got added to the list. Pole dancer was on that list too. But I will save that story for another book.

When Will I Be Loved?

Whether you prefer the Everly Brothers' version or Linda Ronstadt's version of the song, the question remains the same—When will I be loved?

Originally, this was slated to be my very last "Mis-Matched to Miss Matched" article. I even completely cancelled my online subscriptions. But, life happened as I was making plans, and I had to change the title, add all new content, and sadly, alter the ending.

I met an unusual man who proudly proclaimed he was into minimalistic living.

I replied, "Okay. I can deal with that. I don't need a bunch of electronic gadgets or toys. I'm content with what I have now."

Then he declared, "I will never live in a house again. Ever."

At first, I thought he was joking. I laughed. "But if the woman you married had a house, then you could move into her house."

"No. I will never live in a house again, no matter who owns it."

Still thinking he was pulling my leg, I asked, "So, you'd rather pay rent and have nothing to show for it? Even if you have a viable alternative?"

"I'm committed to minimalistic living."

At that point, he showed me a picture of the living space in his apartment. There was one chair and one lamp. That's it. Nothing else. I'm assuming there was a bed somewhere. Perhaps not.

I commented, "There's no place for visitors to sit."

"I don't want visitors. Ever."

Shaking my head in disbelief, I said, "I have visitors a few times a year."

"No. I won't allow visitors."

"It's just my parents."

"No. Visitors don't ever leave."

"My parents do. They have busy social lives. They don't want to stay here."

"No. No visitors ever."

"They're my parents."

"No. No exceptions."

Then, he finally admitted that he was unemployed. That might explain the whole minimalistic living thing. It was more out of necessity than principle.

Don't get me wrong, I believe there are times in one's life when living in an apartment or a condo makes sense. I'm not at that point yet. I like the peace, quiet, and privacy of a house. No noise from upstairs or downstairs neighbors. I like independent living. Thank you, very much.

My next suitor was a daredevil and a party animal. He was the most ruggedly handsome guy I had agreed to meet thus far. He entertained me with lots of stories about drinking, drugs, and death-defying feats. I could have done without some of the drinking and drug stories. However, the daredevil stories were fascinating. I was impressed he had lived this long. But I was not looking for Evil Knievel.

The gentleman who followed was the polar opposite of Mr. Knievel. He was nice, polite, and conservative. But he was as boring as they come. I do not go on dates to hear myself talk. I want the guy to tell me about himself and engage in a conversation. How can I get to know someone when he does not speak? He was the king of awkward silences.

Check, please!

The entrepreneur who followed had interesting ideas concerning food. He was thinking about becoming a vegetarian. That's fine with me, although, I would not become one myself. Granted, I do not eat a lot of meat. But every once and awhile, I need a nice juicy steak!

As the conversation progressed, he said, "If we live together, you can't have chocolate or sweets in the house."

Wait. What? I can't have chocolate in my own house?

I pictured myself sneaking out of the house under the cover of darkness. I would wear a black trench coat and escape to a clandestine meeting with a perfect, medium-cooked filet mignon and a warm, gooey, decadent chocolate dessert.

My car's glove box would be under lock and key. I would have installed a temperature controlling device to prevent my Hershey's bars (with almonds) from becoming misshapen melted blobs.

Oh the humanity!

Lest I forget, let me throw in a not-so-random observation. Fall must be the time of year for men to be exhausted and take mandatory naps. Three, count them, three different guys fell asleep during dates while watching movies. I am not referring to a quick head nod. I am talking about deep sleep, complete with snoring. Hard to discuss the movie afterward when one of us slept through it. Anyway …

Late in the year, I thought I had finally found, "The One." He was good-looking, kind, fun-loving, generous, and financially secure, among other things. And did I mention he was hot? God had finally answered my prayers.

I liked his kids, and they liked me. And I quote, "She is the best one we've ever met."

High praise coming from a teen and pre-teen. When they hugged me, they meant it. They were not giving me the I'm-being-forced-to-hug-you type of hugs. They were great kids. Everything was picture perfect.

The two of us went on a vacation. We saw two Cirque du Soleil shows, toured several exhibits, enjoyed tons of delicious food and decadent desserts, and took a romantic gondola ride. It was fantastic, and we had a great time. Or so I thought.

A few days after we returned, he called me on the phone and broke up with me. Just like that. Out of the blue. No indication of any issue or problem prior to the phone call.

He said, "You didn't do anything wrong. You didn't say or do anything wrong. It's me. I haven't been in a relationship in a long time. I thought I was ready. But I'm not. I'm sorry."

Stunned and dumbfounded, I asked, "Do you want to slow things down and not see each other as much?"

His answer was plain and simple. "No. I just want to end it. I'm sorry."

I will spare you the crying details and the amount of Kleenex I went through nursing my broken heart. Again.

As I mentioned, this was intended to be the last article in my dating series. I completely cancelled my online dating memberships. We had discussed marriage.

I apologize to you, dear readers. There was no way for me to make the last section funny and entertaining.

However, I am choosing to look at the bright side. The relationship was wonderful while it lasted. And I got a really great vacation out of it.

I will leave you with the words of Alfred Lord Tennyson: "'Tis better to have loved and lost than never to have loved at all."

A Shape-Shifter, A Sex Addict, and A Dominant Male

As I mentioned in the last chapter, I cancelled my online subscriptions. Yet, after a few months, like a moth to a flame, I went back. Some of the old familiar faces were still there. But there was a new batch of men from which to choose. This chapter will be about the new breed of online guys.

A man, claiming to be 50, contacted me. However, he looked more like 65. In his first e-mail, he said, "Science and technology are also a substantial part of my life, I'm on my third 3D printer as well as having machining capabilities in my garage. I do have one minor abnormality I should probably tell you about antlers yep antlers thought they were horns but they fall off every spring. Kind of sucks in the fall I have to stay in, damn hunters. I like watching football so it's not all bad. Right now I look perfectly normal but in a month or so they're start to grow back. I've had people think there were tumors but nope antlers. It could be worse just ask my brother Rudy."

Do I want to know what he was making with those 3D printers?

What's frightening was that he actually wore out two of them. He was on his third. Ponder that a minute.

As far as shape-shifting into a reindeer is concerned, reindeers do not turn me on. If he had said he could morph into a unicorn, then *that* would have piqued my interest. I could have definitely made it work with a unicorn!

The next cad was 60 and lived in Florida.

His opening line was insulting. "Your profile is very intriguing…but you might be too young and immature for me."

I agreed with the young part. The insult on my maturity was uncalled for and revealed a great deal about him as a man. Do women respond to that? Does anyone? Oh, the things I wanted to write! But I took the high road.

I responded, "Thank you for your interest. But the age difference would be an issue. I wish you luck finding a match."

"Same to you. The age diff would likely be an insurmountable challenge. Maybe you will mature. Or not…likely."

It's obvious he was a verbal abuser. I can only imagine what insults he would hurl in person.

The next guy's profile stated he was 48. In reality, he was over 50. He admitted that during our first phone call. He said no one responded to him when he claimed his real age. He also told me that he had an additional child that he did not include in his profile. His older kids were teenagers. But he had a fling with a 20-something, and now he had a toddler too. He claimed that putting his youngest child's age on his profile turned off women.

I agreed with that assessment. However, he failed to understand that lying, even by omission, was a bigger problem than completing his profile honestly.

He boasted about his high IQ and his accomplishments. His accomplishments were many, and his drive will ensure additional contributions to his field of study. I was sufficiently impressed.

Things went askew during the second phone call when he started describing his sex life.

Brace yourself, people.

He claimed to have had sex with over 300 women. No, that's *not* a typo. He liked having a harem. Back in the day, he had approximately ten women in his harem at a time. They all knew about each other. In his mind, that made it acceptable.

He stated, "I expect sex on the first date. My success rate is 87%."

Stunned, I answered, "I would never have sex with someone on a first date."

"Then you wouldn't get a second date."

"That's fine because I wouldn't want to go out with someone who demands sex before we even know each other."

He bragged, "And I never use protection. I'm allergic to latex."

Disgusted, I replied, "I can't even imagine all of the diseases you have or have had."

He shrugged it off. "Nothing that a pill or a shot in the ass couldn't fix."

Repulsed, I said, "You've got to be kidding me."

Then he admitted, "Well, I do have herpes. But everybody has herpes."

I argued, "No, they don't! I don't have herpes!"

Nonchalantly, he commented, "It's nothing anyway."

Oh … My … God!

Then he decided to tell me the craziest thing he had done sexually.

Trust me, it was *bad. Really bad. Gross, disgusting bad.* Bad enough to make my body involuntarily shiver as I covered my mouth in disgust. I am glad I heard it over the phone. I can only imagine what my reaction would have been in person.

When I refused to meet him, he became angry. I was worried about catching something just being in the same room with him.

The next "conversation" was via texting. He proceeded to insult me at length and used statistics to justify his generalizations about me. He pontificated on and on about how I was the one with problems, not him.

I argued, "You're way off base. I'm not an ice princess nor am I mentally ill. I'm just not interested in being part of your wham-bam-thank-you-ma'am harem club."

Ignoring me, he continued, "I know my assessment of you is correct. I can base my conclusions on my experience. Since my sample size is so large, statistically, my results and conclusions are valid."

I pointed out, "But the women you attract are not a good cross-section of the entire female population. Your results are skewed because of it."

"No. I'm always right about women."

I ended the conversation.

The irony was that I felt sorry for him. Several women in his life disappointed him early on. The trend continued, and in essence, broke him. He was unfulfilled and angry at the world.

Believe it or not, I said a prayer for him. He's never going to be happy travelling down this current road. Hopefully, he eventually finds peace.

The next candidate was a local artist.

His first e-mail read: "Marry me."

Jokingly, I replied, "If you didn't have dogs, I'd consider it."

"I don't have dogs. It's a typo."

Technically, it was not a typo. You have to pick a selection from a menu. If you do not have pets, you skip the section. Then he sent me a list of his deal breakers.

"Heres my deal breakers…what are yours?

1.) Alpha personalities (which are usually validated through tough hypervigilance, and worldly experience) then usually manifest out into a reactionary temperamental disposition which culminates in "not so good" communication, hurt feelings, and an emotional withdrawal from the gentle, nurturing, tenderness and understanding that a relationship needs to galvanize a good foundation.

2.) Country Music (love the lyrics, don't like the redundant "twang") i.e. it's too "traditional" and not "out of the box-ish".

3.) Tacky low-rent tattoos

4.) Competitiveness

5.) OCD (obsessive-compulsive disorder

6.) Manics and hypomania

7.) A foul mouth (the "f" word etc)

8.) Slow-progressive-placated functional alcoholism (when a person is slowly on their way to an addiction through self-medicating with liquor).

9.) Anything KARDASHIAN. (The Kardashians represent a very self-entitled, self preserving, materialistic, ostentatious way to be as a human being.)

Everything else I can work with ……………. giggles"

I admit, I agree with most of the items on his list. However, the two that were issues for me were "alpha personalities" and "competitiveness."

He sent me a link to an article he wrote about women. He wrote, in part, "… one of the most revealing and toxic awakenings in our culture today: The emergence of the Alpha personality in women and it's pervasive influence in the symbiotic growth of the union of woman and man."

Wow! And double wow! I just got thrown back to the 1950s. And the editor in me wanted to correct his errors.

I did not lose to boys on purpose when I was young, and I am certainly not going to start doing that now.

I was taught to always do my best. That way you challenge yourself and others. Sometimes you win. Sometimes you lose. Not everyone goes home with a trophy. It also taught us sportsmanship and how to win and lose gracefully.

The competitor in me could not resist responding to the notion of acquiescing at all times. I typed, "As far as being competitive goes, I won't lose to a man on purpose. If a guy's ego is that fragile, then he's not for me."

I knew his reply would be negative because I was goading him. *Oh, shame on me!*

"i really dont care for your statement … this tells me theres an unecessary competitive streak in you that im not gonna dig…take care"

That was perfectly fine by me. The last time I checked, the year was 2016.

I believe that some friendly competition is perfectly acceptable in any healthy relationship. Remember to always celebrate each other's strengths and triumphs. Do not dwell on the negatives or weaknesses. Build each other up!

To borrow the Army's old slogan, "Be All That You Can Be." Life is too short to do anything else.

Drunk and Drunker

This article's dating tales revolve around two men and their love affairs with alcohol.

The first guy passed the preliminaries. However, when I met him, there were a few red flags. Nevertheless, I ignored my better judgment and went on several dates with him.

He declared that he worked out four or five times a week, lived a healthy lifestyle, and was going to lose more weight. He had already lost 100 pounds.

Although I did not observe him making any healthy food selections, it was his drinking that bothered me. He did not stop at one or two drinks.

If you have been following me through this journey, you know I am a one-drink person when I am out, and I am the designated driver. I will not get into a car with someone who is legally drunk.

During our last date, I met him at his favorite restaurant. This place carried a special type of wine just for him. I learned that on our first date. That was a giant red flag, which I chose to overlook.

He greeted me with a hello kiss. Then he proceeded to tell me how sick he was and how horrible he felt. The congestion in his chest was terrible. He held his chest and coughed. It sounded like bronchitis to me.

Backing away, I reacted, "Yikes! No more kisses for you until you're well."

He replied, "Oh, you're one of those."

One of those? If you mean people who don't want you contaminating them with all of your respiratory infection germs, yes, I'm one of those. Be considerate. Good Lord!

I sighed as I sat across from him.

Then he coughed and coughed, without covering his mouth.

I am positive I cringed as I shifted to the right. At least that way he was not coughing directly on me. I mentioned that he should be coughing into his elbow.

Eventually, he covered his mouth with his hand. Then, he wanted me to hold that hand.

Are you trying to get me sick on purpose?

Thank God, I had antibacterial wipes.

While he enjoyed his third glass of wine, he saw I was agitated. He asked, "What's on your mind?"

Oh, buddy, you just asked the wrong question. I don't think you really want to know. I'm thinking I'm going to catch this plague you have. And your drinking is bothering me. But since you asked …

"The amount you drink bothers me. Every time we've gone out, except one time, you've had a lot to drink. Not just one or two glasses of wine, but multiple glasses. I'm concerned."

"I'm not an alcoholic."

"Do you drink every day?"

"I usually don't go out during the week."

Not sure what that had to do with the price of tea in China, I replied, "Well, I won't ride with a person who's legally drunk. If you're always going to drink like this, I will always have to drive."

Defensively, he argued, "I am not drunk! Do I look drunk? Do I act drunk? Am I slurring my words?"

"No." *Because you have built up a tolerance.*

He continued, "My friends drink hard liquor. I drink wine. It's better. We're here every Friday and Saturday night drinking at the bar. They drink hard liquor. I drink my wine."

Every Friday and Saturday? Drunk is still drunk, dude. Any cop will tell you that. As will a blood alcohol test.

I stated, "It doesn't matter what you're drinking. Alcohol is alcohol."

"It's just wine. And now you're making me uncomfortable and self-conscious."

"Sorry, you asked, and I had to say something because it's making me uncomfortable."

Dismissively, he responded, "You're making something out of nothing. I'm not an alcoholic. You don't drink wine, so you don't understand."

What's there to understand? Wine contains alcohol last time I checked.

He stopped the waitress and asked for another glass of wine.

Are you freaking kidding me? Way to show me you don't have a drinking problem.

She emptied the contents of the bottle into his glass. That was glass number four.

As he drank, I got the you're-not-the-boss-of-me look and vibe.

I shook my head and ate my dinner.

I was not trying to be the boss of anyone. However, drinking and driving is a serious issue. And I refuse to be with a man who drinks to excess all the time.

Then he said, "Next you're going to tell me I can't ride my motorcycle without a helmet."

Heavy sigh.

Annoyed, I said, "No, you can do whatever you want."

Obviously, because nothing I say matters anyway.

After he drained his glass, he asked the waitress for yet another glass.

She answered, "I emptied the bottle last time. Do you want me to open a new bottle for you?"

"Yes."

If you are counting with me, this was glass number five.

Finally, dinner was over.

After that evening, my texts to him were short.

He texted, "So I'm assuming by your lack of communication and enthusiasm, you've lost interest and can't get over my evil wine drinking ways."

You guessed right! That and your complete disregard for my welfare by spewing all over me and for not understanding why I would not want to put my life into the hands of someone who was legally drunk.

I wrote, "You disregarded my concern completely. I understood finishing the glass in front of you. Then you had her open another bottle. And you got defensive and dismissive. I can't handle being with someone who drinks 5 glasses of wine in that short amount of time and disregards my feelings."

"Actually it was 3 glasses and that hardly makes me an alcoholic…I wasn't trying to dismiss you by ordering another glass but I was trying to make a point that I'm 52 years old and I'm pretty set in my ways."

I was not going to argue about the number of glasses or about anything else for that matter. I was drinking water and clearly counted five glasses of wine.

From now on, I really need to pay attention to those pesky red flags!

A friend attempted to help me in my quest for "Mr. Right." She invited a friend, an extremely wealthy businessman, to meet us for drinks and a light dinner. We were sitting at the bar when he showed up three sheets to the wind.

That was extremely disappointing. And did I mention that he looked older than my parents? So, he had nothing working in his favor.

I was polite at first. Alas, after I had heard the exact same story for the third time, I was mentally done. I ignored him the best I could, but he kept hanging on me.

I caught the eye of a young, handsome guy a few seats away. I gave him my "help me" look. He laughed and looked away.

Damn!

Without another option, I disappeared to the ladies' room. I stayed in there entirely too long. When I returned, "Tipsy," was sitting in my chair.

Thank you, Jesus!

I quickly sat next to the handsome guy.

He looked up at me and smiled.

I smiled back. "I need you to save me."

"I know. I saw the look."

Exasperated, I threw up my hands. "But you didn't save me."

"Trust me, we've got your back."

"We?"

"As soon as you left for the bathroom, I watched your drink. I was convinced that guy was going to put something in it."

"Really?"

"Yes. He looks like that kind of guy. A real creeper."

I laughed.

He continued, "And the bartender is watching out for you too. And the piano guy hasn't taken his eyes off you all night."

"Good to know I'm covered. Thank you."

"Don't mention it."

He wore a wedding band. Of course, the gorgeous ones are always married!

I said, "I know that you're married, and I'm not hitting on you. I just need someone to talk to until he leaves."

"No problem."

We had a nice conversation. When his wife and teenage daughter showed up, he introduced me to them. He explained the story. His daughter got wide-eyed when he said he thought the guy was going to drug my drink.

Glad I could provide a teachable moment. Hopefully, she'll remember this when she goes to parties.

This nice family even asked me if I wanted to join them at a booth for dinner.

"No, thank you. I don't want to intrude."

"If you change your mind …"

I shook their hands. "Thank you."

My friend and Tipsy went out to smoke.

The bartender said, "You look like you could use that dessert now."

I nodded. "Yes, please."

I ate my chocolate dessert and talked to the bartender and the pianist.

Finally, it was time to leave.

My leather jacket was on the back of the businessman's chair. He insisted on helping me with it. As he slipped on the coat, he commented, "Oh, the leather is so soft."

Then he reached around and grabbed my right breast.

Let me tell you something, dear readers. I have never, ever hit anyone. But at that moment, I really wanted to punch him. It took every ounce of strength I had within me not to hit him.

I hear you screaming, "Why the hell not? Hit him! Slap him! For God's sake, knee him!"

I was almost a head taller than him. He had been drinking steadily since he arrived. So, he was drunk as a skunk and unsteady on his feet. I knew that if I struck him, his sorry geriatric ass would go down hard, very hard. And with my luck, he would have broken a hip. Then, he and his army of lawyers would have had me arrested.

Friends, I would not do well in jail. Not for a single minute. Instead, I will let karma take care of him. He will get what's coming to him in the end.

In the meantime, I might kill him off in one of my books. Or not. I guess you will have to buy my next novel to find out.

Not So Helpful Dating Advice

As my quest for a boyfriend continues, many readers have offered well-intentioned advice. I appreciate their suggestions. However, I believe some suggestions are slightly off the mark. The most common advice I received: Go to church.

Okay, let's try to work out some strategies for trolling for a man at church. I am sure the nuns would disapprove. But Pope Francis seems pretty progressive. So what the heck, why not?

Plan A: Be a greeter.

I could check out the men entering alone or with children in tow. After checking their fingers for wedding rings, I would observe how well-behaved their children were or were not. Guys with screaming banshees would be eliminated immediately. Then I could transform into an usher for the remaining bachelors and escort them to nice, hard, wooden pews, chatting them up the entire time.

Plan B: Hijack the lector.

The lector in most churches also reads the weekly announcements.

I would snatch the list and race to the lectern for an eagle eye view of the congregation. I would insert my plight of trying to find a guy who is husband material in between announcing the second collection for our sister parish in (insert name of Third World Country here) and reminding everyone to come out and enjoy Bingo night. Interested parties should see me in the Narthex after Mass.

Plan C: Determine how Catholic these men really are.

During Mass, I could position myself on the end of a pew that has a good line of sight to most of the church. I would see who knows the words to the prayers without having to look at the Missalette and who at least attempts to sings the songs. Failure in either category jettisons them from consideration.

Plan D: Be the guest homilist.

Perhaps the real guest speaker accidentally locks himself/herself in the bride's room or the crying room, allowing me to speak instead. My topic would be about finding your one true love, making it clear that I am one of those people still looking. Any man who nods off would be scratched off the list. Again, interested parties should check me out in the Narthex after Mass.

Plan E: Locate Mr. Moneybags.

I could volunteer to pass the basket around at Offertory, a.k.a. The Presentation of the Gifts. I could sort through the envelopes looking at donation amounts. And lucky me, I have extra time because of that special second collection for our sister parish in that Third World country. The largest donor wins!

Plan F: Glad-hand.

I would scope out the best candidates based on Plans A through E. At the Sign of Peace, I would dart around the church and shake those guys' hands, hoping for a spark when our eyes meet. Wimpy handshakes, clammy handshakes, and God-forbid, sticky handshakes would be deemed unacceptable.

Plan G: Check out their jeans.

During Communion, I could check out their rear ends as they file up to the priest to receive the holy sacrament. Once I selected the men with the nicest derrieres, after Mass, I would hand them a bulletin with my name and phone number on it.

All perfect plans, right? *Not.*

That settles it. Trolling for a boyfriend during a Catholic Mass is not feasible, not to mention, it's just wrong! And I would probably have to go to Confession because of it. Imagine how that would go.

"Bless me, Father, for I have sinned. It's been thirty-two years since my last confession."

Hey, don't judge me. The only thing I ever had to confess was arguing with my brother. I was a goody two-shoes. Ask anybody who knows me. My penance was always one Our Father, three Hail Marys, and a Glory Be.

If I had to confess to a priest today, I would confess to occasionally swearing and killing off characters in my books, who may or may not represent people in real life who have pissed me off.

I think God understands why I do both.

You Want Me To Do What?

There were a few stories that I did not divulge on my blog concerning men with fetishes. After my encounter with the crossdresser, I decided if a man made it to a second date, I would ask if he had any fetishes.

The first man to confess his fetish to me was an artist who lived in Illinois. His artwork was absolutely brilliant. After viewing his portfolio online, I had to meet him. He was one of two people who I agreed to meet who lived out of state. We met at a restaurant that was halfway between our cities.

He was visibly nervous. I tried to put him at ease. He eventually relaxed. We had a good enough time to warrant a second date. I offered to drive to his town to check it out. It was a small, quiet town with the usual strip malls and a park.

After lunch, I asked if he had any fetishes. He quickly responded that he did.

Surprised, I asked, "What is it?"

"I have a nylon fetish."

Curious, I followed up. "Nylon as a material, or rope, or what?"

"Pantyhose."

First you have to realize that after being in the manufacturing world for over two decades, I was thinking nylon material. Pantyhose didn't cross my mind. I never called them nylons. We always called them stockings or pantyhose.

I confirmed, "You would want me to wear pantyhose."

"All the time would be great, but especially during sex."

He showed me pictures on his cell phone of women in pantyhose. His favorite brand was an expensive one from Italy. Those women's legs looked fantastic. The stockings had a sheen to them that made their legs glow and glisten.

He reassured me that it did not matter what type I wore. It could be cheap ones from Sears or wherever.

I haven't worn a pair of pantyhose in years, but I had what I thought was a better and sexier option. "How about thigh highs?"

"No. They're not as good as pantyhose."

Huh. Well, stockings do make my legs look better by covering up those ugly spider veins. I might be able to live with this fetish.

"Okay. I could wear pantyhose on occasion."

By his facial expression, I could tell there was more to it. I inquired, "Am I the only one wearing pantyhose?"

Shaking his head, he replied, "No."

"Okay. So, I would be wearing them, and you would be wearing them."

"Yes. Exactly. Particularly during sex."

"Obviously, the crotches would be cut out."

"Well, yours would be. Mine wouldn't."

Hold on a minute. Although I tried not to picture this scenario, my mind could not help itself. I imagined a lot of chaffing and static electricity building up, but not a lot else. My facial expression betrayed me.

He said, "I'm guessing that would be a problem for you."

Perplexed, I said, "I don't understand how that would work if you're bound up in the nylons."

I never got an explanation. He became defensive and overly-sensitive to everything that was said after that. I attempted to be as understanding and accepting as possible. But he threw up walls faster than anyone I have ever met. Then, he shut down completely.

I don't consider the day a total loss. I like road trips, and that was a town I had never visited.

The next man was in the entertainment industry and a world traveler. This bald, clean-shaven guy dressed nicely and was very polite. He had awesome stories. We went to a concert, museums, and little hole-in-the-wall places to eat. After several dates, I asked him the fetish question.

He smiled. "I would love for you to shave me."

I am not shy about admitting that I hate shaving myself, let alone perform that dreaded loathsome task on someone else.

I responded, "I don't think that's a good idea. I wouldn't want to cut your face."

He smirked. "I wasn't talking about my face."

I knew from his intonation and body language, he was talking about way down yonder.

He added, "And I want you to do it with a straight razor."

God, no!

I protested, "No way. Seriously, your life would be in danger if I attempted that. I have never touched a straight razor in my life. I cut myself with a safety razor. There's no way I'm going near your family jewels with a deadly weapon."

In a reassuring tone, he replied, "I'll teach you how. It's easy. You'll get the hang of it in no time."

Why couldn't his fetish have involved shaving me? What an enormous time-saver that would be if someone would shave my legs and other delicate areas!

I declined, "I wouldn't want to risk it."

Inching closer, he whispered, "You'll be fine."

Standing my ground, I said, "I'll be fine, but you won't. Trust me. There's no way I could do that."

"Sure you can."

"Nope, not in a million years."

Then there was an artistic guy who had a bondage fetish. I always thought that bondage, sadomasochism, and sex were a package deal. He informed me that was not always the case. He admitted that he sometimes used bondage during sex. However, overall, he claimed a great deal of his bondage-play had nothing to do with sex or inflicting pain.

He described the special rope he used that didn't leave marks on his subjects. But what really got him revved up was showing me pictures of women tied up. They were hog-tied in the most complicated and elaborate macramé projects I had ever seen. Some of the work was exquisite. The knotting work literally took hours upon hours.

Well, being tied up, down, or any other way is not on my bucket list. And I can't imagine sitting in that outrageous position for hours while he tied knot after knot in a slow, tedious fashion. If I didn't die of boredom, the foot cramps and back spasms would be torturous.

I challenged him. "Making someone sit in a fixed, extremely uncomfortable position for hours on end equates to inflicting pain in my book."

"I'm not hitting them. And the ropes won't hurt them unless they struggle and try to get out of them."

"How about if they have to go to the bathroom?"

"Sometimes, I'll make allowances."

Aren't you a peach? Then I asked if he used a mannequin or an inflatable stand-in to do any of the work. In my mind, that would maximize his knot-tying time and minimize the boring, uncomfortable, stay-in-this-position-for-hours time for his subject.

You should have seen the look he gave me. Evidently, I was insane for mentioning it.

I asked, "So after you tie the women up, do you let them tie you up?"

Definitively, he replied, "No. Never."

"Never?"

"Never. I won't let anyone tie me up."

"Why?"

"Because I said so."

Apparently, what's good for the goose is not good for the gander!

I wanted to get help for the next guy. I am warning you now, if you are easily offended or do not want to read about what many consider to be deviant sexual behavior, please skip this section. Go to the next story. This means you, Mom and Dad!

I am not writing this for shock value. This was just part of the crazy online dating journey that I experienced.

A younger man contacted me via e-mail. When I viewed his profile, I had to google half of the words I read. Honestly. I had no idea what many of them meant.

From what I could gather, he was looking for a relationship with a dominant woman who would control every aspect of his life, and I mean right down to the minutia, including bathroom breaks.

He wanted a woman to physically, verbally, and sexually abuse him. He even detailed his favorite forms of torture. Many involved feces, urine, and/or blood. He also wanted this woman to restrain him and force him to watch her having S&M sexual encounters with men and women. He also insisted that his genitalia be kept in a physical metal cage, around the clock, that could only be unlocked by this sadistic woman.

I wondered what horrible things this man endured as a child to end up this way. I felt so sad for this tortured soul. This was not playful role-playing. This was hard core stuff.

I understand there are many people in the world who practice this type of behavior. Fortunately, I have lived a sheltered life. For that, I am thankful. I could not imagine living a life filled with such abuse, violence, self-loathing, and self-destruction.

My e-mail reply was short. "I am not the type of woman you are looking for." In truth, I wanted to type a lot more. Instead, I said a prayer for him.

The Time I Completely Lost My Mind

My house was in desperate need of some miscellaneous repairs. I contacted a local handyman to give me an estimate. He was an older guy, close to my dad's age. He gave me a good estimate, and we scheduled a week for the work to be done.

On the first day of repairs, I decided to clean out closets. So, when the doorbell rang, I was dressed in an old ratty sweatshirt and ill-fitting jeans. No makeup either. I wasn't looking to impress the old guy.

I opened the door. There stood a tall, younger guy. I wanted to die. I know he was speaking because his lips were moving. But his deep hazel eyes had me entranced. For all I knew, he might have been a serial killer, but I let him in the house anyway.

Finally, the rational side of my brain kicked in. He would be doing the prep work, drywall, and painting portions of the job. Most of the work was in the master bathroom.

As he worked, we chatted. He was a musician and an artist. He loved hiking and parks. We were so caught up in our conversation, we didn't hear the old guy enter the house. As a result, when he appeared, I jumped and screamed.

The old guy said, "I rang the doorbell and knocked. Guess you didn't hear me."

Whoops! Guess not.

Then I did a crazy ditzy thing, I found more work for the younger guy to do. He seemed more than happy to oblige.

During a moment alone, he asked, "Would you like to go out for coffee sometime?"

I confessed, "Yes. And if you didn't ask me, I was going to ask you."

He smiled.

Then the old guy reappeared. I hadn't had time to give the other guy my number. They had another job to do, and the old guy was trying to get the young one to leave.

I made up another problem and asked the handsome guy to look at it. That's when I slipped him one of my business cards. He discretely put it in his pocket.

He began texting me later that day. He returned to finish the drywall and painting the following day. We sat on my bathroom floor and literally watched paint dry. The conversation was really deep and fascinating. His creativity was off the charts. He had ambitious plans for the future.

We went on a few dates. He was ten years younger than me, but he looked older. I invited him to one of my book signings. He showed up, and my fellow female authors were stunned. Did I forget to mention his blue hair, the myriad of visible tattoos, and multiple piercings?

Most of the tattoos were dark subject matter. I asked him what the tattoos represented. There were only three that had any significance. The rest held no meaning. He thought they were cool and wanted his arms completely covered. I found that bizarre.

If I was going to withstand medieval torture to imprint something permanently on my body, it would have to have the utmost significance. Anyway …

Let's just say when the ladies met him, they thought I had lost my mind and told me so. Instantly, I gained two more mothers. They didn't forbid me to see him again, but they came close.

In the meantime, he offered to feature me on his podcast. He had a show and used an alias. Authors use aliases, so that didn't faze me.

I looked him up online to check out his web pages and podcasts. That's when I discovered the true extent of his alter ego. Mind you, he had only shown me his contemplative, artistic, musical, gentle, nature-loving side. What I saw online was a heavy drinking, party animal surrounded by a scary bunch of people in trashed out rooms. No smiling happy people in these pictures, just angry expressions with pierced tongues sticking out and middle fingers on display, or unconscious people on couches surrounded by others who appeared higher than kites. Other pictures showed them defacing public property.

Talk about disappointing. I guess I shouldn't have been too surprised. It's not like my new moms didn't warn me.

In a text, I mentioned that I found him online. He didn't respond to the text. Instead, he freaked out and blocked me from his Facebook accounts.

Too late, buddy. I already saw every idiotic, stupid, ugly thing about you.

Oh well. That's okay. I really didn't want any more lectures from my new moms anyway. The worst part was that the repair work was left unfinished.

Note to self: Don't date the hired help.

Over the River and Through the Woods

After deflecting another bunch of noncontenders, a more interesting prospect contacted me. He was in marketing. His personality appeared bigger than life.

Our first date involved lunch and a tour of the venue for one of his upcoming events. The venue was a multimillion-dollar mansion, often rented out for a variety of functions. It was positively spectacular. I wish I could describe all of its unique features. However, if I did, then it would be easy to identify the house, and even possibly, this bachelor. Thus, no detailed descriptions. But if I owned this house with its amenities and accoutrements, I would never have to leave the grounds.

Although, I would fire the cleaning staff. They did an abysmal job. Some windowsills and bookcases hadn't been dusted since the Clinton administration.

On a whim, he decided I needed a tour of the grounds. It had rained, so the ground was muddy. He reassured me we would be on a path. Well, he lost the path, and we ended up in a muddy area. We were so off-course, when we reached a stream, the bridge was nowhere in sight. However, there were rocks in the stream.

He bounded over the rocks and held out his hand to help me across.

Since my pretty, black, medium-heeled boots were already caked in mud, I figured if I fell in, at least the mud would be washed off.

Miraculously, I made it across, to another muddy field. We trudged along until we reached a playhouse, long abandoned. We climbed a wooden ladder to the upper deck. The view of the river and woods was beautiful from this vantage point. And I bet the young boys who played in this miniature house didn't appreciate the view.

The trek back toward the house was half-path, half-wilderness. My boots had seen much better days. He suggested we go to one of the out-buildings.

Sure, why not? Maybe we could catch a safari adventure while we were at it.

In that building, he washed his shoes and my boots. Very nice of him.

We went on a couple of "normal" dates. However, he was too much of a partier for me. He spent most of his time going to parties and bars. All of his online pictures had the same theme—a bunch of women hanging all over him.

No, thank you.

I only travelled out of state twice during this dating journey. One of the times, I drove three hours to Ohio. This gentleman was intelligent, soft-spoken, an avid cyclist, and an author of eloquent poetry. He drove here for our first date. So, I drove to him for our second date.

When I arrived, he greeted me with a dozen roses. It was a lovely gesture. I love roses. After lunch, he gave me a quick tour of the city. Then, we went to an art museum and his Hindu temple. It was my first visit to a Hindu temple. It was beautiful. I tried to absorb as much as I could about the various gods. Then, we had dinner at a quiet restaurant. It was a perfect day, activity-wise.

We talked for a couple of weeks after that. However, the distance proved too much of an obstacle for me. He was a wonderful guy. But not being able to spend quality time together on a regular basis, I felt he was more of a friend. And unfortunately, because he was Indian, there were things about him that reminded me of my ex-husband. Alas, that was the end of our story.

The Sound of Silence

This chapter's subject of interest is a handsome 42-year-old professional. He was downright yummy, intelligent, and funny. At first, he acted attentive and eager to please. He even sang to me while we slow danced. I was in heaven. It was a romantic dream come true! Slow dancing and singing! Just imagine it!

After a few weeks, I felt him pulling away. When I showed up for a date all dressed up, he did not say that I looked nice. I complimented him on how good he looked, and he just said, "Thanks."

As the evening progressed, I knew something was amiss. We had always been open and honest with our communication, so I decided to say something.

I said, "I'm a little confused. I need you to be more demonstrative. I don't know what you're thinking or what you're feeling. I'm falling in love with you. But I have no idea what you're feeling toward me."

Dead silence. For what seemed an eternity.

Finally, he replied, "I'm happy and content. Can't that be enough?"

Um, I don't think so. I'm falling in love with you, and you're just happy and content? I'm going to lose my mind.

I thought maybe there was something I could do to improve his "happy and content" status. I offered, "I've asked you to do that for me. What do you want me to do for you?"

He answered, "I wish you would appreciate silence more. It's like you're a radio talk show host, and you don't want there to be any dead air time."

Okey dokey then.

That was where that conversation ended. He acted as if everything was fine and cuddled with me.

In the following days, I attempted to keep my side of the conversations shorter. I thought I did very well. But he pulled away even more. He stopped responding to my texts and stopped calling with no explanation.

That brings us up to yesterday. I started out with an almost flat tire. Thank goodness I got to the tire place before I did any damage to the wheel. Then, that same car conked out at Auto Zone. The battery died. Changing a car battery in a parking lot was just about the most fun I could have had on a humid 90°F day. And did I mention this day also would have been my twenty-third wedding anniversary? Anyway …

Since the day was already lousy, and after two days of no communication from my boyfriend, I texted him, "Since you've been logging in to Facebook, but you haven't contacted me in two days, I'm guessing you're breaking up with me."

He texted back, "It's just not going to work. I have nowhere the time you need. I have no plans to get married soon if ever …"

I will spare you all of the texting details. He went on to say that he thought he was over his ex-girlfriend, but he wasn't. I had a feeling that was a big part of it. He started dating way too soon after his breakup.

The marriage issue would definitely have been a problem. I am not dating in order to date a man forever.

He texted, "I want you to know that this isn't like there's something 'wrong with you'…This is a compatibility thing. I literally have very little free time and it was clear that I was not going to let go emotionally like you need."

I have to admit he was right about being incompatible in the long run. Honestly, I don't know how long I could have kept up the "be more quiet" thing. But the breakup still hurts. And I will miss the slow dancing and being serenaded.

Now I was late for my neighbor's moving celebration. I put on my happy face and went. He and I moved into the neighborhood, with our former spouses, nineteen years ago. Now, I am the last one standing.

Huh. That seems to be a common theme these days. Well, I don't want to give up. And after I take a moment or two for quiet reflection, I will move on, wherever the path may lead.

I will persevere—one way or another.

Not So Elite

After allowing my online subscription to expire once again, I discovered a more exclusive online website. The people on this high-end dating site were supposedly looking for serious relationships, not hookups.

Well, the majority of matches were out of state. I can not say that I was surprised. Very few men in the state of Indiana share my interests.

Maryland and Washington, D.C. had twenty matches combined. Chicago and its suburbs had fourteen. Michigan showed a little promise with five prospects. Cincinnati rounded out the top five geographical regions with four guys. Only six candidates out of that total did not have pets, and there wasn't an ounce of e-mail chemistry among them.

However, one day, a guy from a different Midwestern state aced the e-mail and phone tests. He was quite a conversationalist, and we discussed a wide variety of topics.

The fly in the ointment was that he lived approximately nine hours away. That would be a very long distance relationship. I was hesitant to pursue this further. Talking on the phone and seeing each other a few times a year was fine for friends, not for a potential husband. He insisted on driving here to meet and inquired about hotels in the area.

Normally, I don't google people prior to meeting them. I prefer to get to know someone organically, rather than rely on what's floating around in cyberspace. However, since he lived so far away, I thought it would be prudent to do so.

He had an uncommon name and was easy to find. What I found was a glaring felony conviction. He had served many years in federal prison.

He had written several songs while in prison. Those were online as well.

The short version of the story is that he attempted to hire a guy to kill his cheating wife. The hired gun ended up being in law enforcement. So, the wife lived to cheat another day, while the jilted husband served hard time.

Needless to say, I cancelled our meeting. He said he understood but wished I could give him a chance. He had found God in prison and was a new man.

Even if I could look past his felonious past, there was no way on God's green earth that my family and friends would tolerate it. My mother's reaction alone would be priceless.

Although I didn't talk to my mother about this particular guy, I imagined the exchange would have gone something like this:

"Suzanne, have you lost your mind? A felon? Who tried to have his wife killed? Did you take stupid pills today or what? There's no way you're meeting him, let alone dating him. That's final."

"But ..."

"But nothing. Are you trying to give me a heart attack or a stroke? Is that your plan? I worry about regular men you date. And now you want to date a convicted felon? I can't say enough Rosaries to protect you. And you know you'd need protection. You would just have to say one wrong or stupid thing, and that would be the end of you. And you know you have a way about you. You'd be dead in no time at all. So, forget it. You're better off alone than dead."

True. I can be stubborn at times. And I have been known to ruffle some feathers in my day. Admittedly, I have enough problems without adding, "dating a convicted felon," to my list. So, I declined his invitation to meet.

Surprisingly, the next day, another match appeared in my inbox. He was my age and lived in Indianapolis. He loved to hike and attend live theater events. Despite that he had a cat and a very young daughter, I was optimistically hopeful. He swore he would be cat-free when he saw me. And his custody agreement was fifty/fifty.

Our first date was impressive. We went to an upscale restaurant for dinner. Then, we attended the musical, *Million Dollar Quartet*.

Million Dollar Quartet is based on a true story about an impromptu jam session with Elvis Presley, Jerry Lee Lewis, Carl Perkins, and Johnny Cash, back in 1956. It was absolutely fantastic! If you haven't seen it, you're missing out on something special! I highly recommend it.

It was an unusually warm evening. We strolled through the nearby park. The second date was a quick lunch. He had his daughter that week. Hence, dinner was out of the question. We planned a third date for the week he did not have his daughter. But it had to be after his daughter's horse riding lesson, or after her soccer practice, or after her soccer game, or after her play.

Confused, I said, "I thought you said your custody agreement is fifty/fifty."

He replied, "She sleeps at my house fifty percent of the time. I still see her every day and attend every one of her riding lessons, practices, and games during the week and on weekends. And we go on vacation every year. I let her pick the destination. Every other year, it's an international destination."

His eyes sparkled when he told me of his daughter's accomplishments and the new activities and sports teams he wanted her to join. Then, he described the exotic places they had already seen and followed up with a list of upcoming vacation adventures for the foreseeable future. He explained how his daughter was an integral part of the planning process.

Reading the writing on the wall, I said, "You really don't have time to date."

"I'm trying to make time."

"This isn't going to work."

"I'm sure we can work something out."

Being the realist I am, I disagreed, "No, I don't think so. Right now, your daughter is the center of your world. And she will be for the next decade or so. You have already planned your father/daughter vacations for the next several years. It's wonderful that you are such an involved father. But I'm looking for someone who wants to spend quality time with me. Alone time. With your current situation, I'm going to be an afterthought. She's used to a team of two. I'll just be the interloper tagging along on your adventures. I won't settle for that. I can't settle for being an outsider looking in. And even if I could put up with that, there's the cat. You're not going to get rid of the cat."

He conceded, "No, I won't get rid of the cat."

"You're a nice guy. But I don't think we can be anything except friends."

Flatly, he responded, "We can't be friends."

"We can't?"

He declared, "No. I can't be friends with anyone I've thought about having a relationship with."

"It's your choice."

He reiterated, "I'm choosing not to be friends."

Well, it's not as if he had time to hang out with a friend anyway!

Déjà Vu

After those two fiascos with the high-end site, I returned to the first website. I'm not convinced it's the best site, but it has become my default position. And lo and behold, there was a face I recognized. I had not seen his profile since I first started this process years ago. We had traded e-mails back then, but our schedules never meshed. He had what equated to two full-time jobs at the time.

Now, he only worked one full-time job. Turned out that he had married someone he found on the site. Now he was divorcing her. Another dissatisfied customer.

We met for dinner and went on a few subsequent dates. He did not have any fetishes. However, he was not divorced yet. The thought of a long-term relationship was nowhere on his radar.

In addition, he was dealing with a great deal of drama from his soon-to-be ex-wife. She basically emptied out his house and left him with nothing except a ton of debt.

Amidst that chaos, his son from a previous marriage announced he was transgender. So, he was struggling with that news. Nevertheless, they were working with a therapist to assist with the transition. I commended him for that.

Since I did not know his child prior to this time, I don't know how the child appeared as a boy. But I can tell you that she was a beautiful girl.

With chaos ruling this guy's life, I knew this would never blossom into a relationship. We parted ways.

There was another guy I recognized but couldn't place. He was selected as my "Match of the Day." When I clicked on his profile, I realized how I knew him. He was my friend's ex-husband. She had introduced me to him months ago, at an open mic night at a café.

I laughed as I told my girlfriend that her ex popped up as a 97% match. Her reaction was unexpected.

She said, "You should go out with him."

Confused, I replied, "Huh? That would be too weird."

Plus, I thought, *She didn't want him, why would I?*

She explained, "I think you guys would be great together. He's got a good job. You're both musicians. And then I wouldn't have to worry about my kids. They like you, and you would be a great stepmother to them."

All true. But dating her ex-husband would be odd. I would start avoiding her because all of us hanging out together would be uncomfortable. Plus, he had two other strikes against him. He had a drinking problem and a cat.

My Twelve Days of Christmas

I penned yet another version of this holiday tune, with my online dating twist. It's destined to be a classic for sure!

On the first day of Christmas, online dating gave to me,
No man worth my membership fee.

On the second day of Christmas, online dating gave to me,
Two e-mails from women,
And no man worth my membership fee.

On the third day of Christmas, online dating gave to me,
Three convicted felons,
Two e-mails from women,
And no man worth my membership fee.

On the fourth day of Christmas, online dating gave to me,
Four fun days in Vegas,
Three convicted felons,

Two e-mails from women,
And no man worth my membership fee.

On the fifth day of Christmas, online dating gave to me,
Five guys who shave more of their bodies than I do,
Four fun days in Vegas,
Three convicted felons,
Two e-mails from women,
And no man worth my membership fee.

On the sixth day of Christmas, online dating gave to me,
Six guys wanting hookups,
Five guys who shave more of their bodies than I do,
Four fun days in Vegas,
Three convicted felons,
Two e-mails from women,
And no man worth my membership fee.

On the seventh day of Christmas, online dating gave to me,
Seven smooth musicians,
Six guys wanting hookups,
Five guys who shave more of their bodies than I do,
Four fun days in Vegas,
Three convicted felons,
Two e-mails from women,
And no man worth my membership fee.

On the eighth day of Christmas, online dating gave to me,
Eight uptight physicians,
Seven smooth musicians,
Six guys wanting hookups,
Five guys who shave more of their bodies than I do,

Four fun days in Vegas,
Three convicted felons,
Two e-mails from women,
And no man worth my membership fee.

On the ninth day of Christmas, online dating gave to me,
Nine dudes from Jersey!?!
Eight uptight physicians,
Seven smooth musicians,
Six guys wanting hookups,
Five guys who shave more of their bodies than I do,
Four fun days in Vegas,
Three convicted felons,
Two e-mails from women,
And no man worth my membership fee.

On the tenth day of Christmas, online dating gave to me,
Ten phony profiles,
Nine dudes from Jersey,
Eight uptight physicians,
Seven smooth musicians,
Six guys wanting hookups,
Five guys who shave more of their bodies than I do,
Four fun days in Vegas,
Three convicted felons,
Two e-mails from women,
And no man worth my membership fee.

On the eleventh day of Christmas, online dating gave to me,
Eleven sushi dinners,
Ten phony profiles,

Nine dudes from Jersey,
Eight uptight physicians,
Seven smooth musicians,
Six guys wanting hookups,
Five guys who shave more of their bodies than I do,
Four fun days in Vegas,
Three convicted felons,
Two e-mails from women,
And no man worth my membership fee.

On the twelfth day of Christmas, online dating gave to me,
Twelve political crackpots,
Eleven sushi dinners,
Ten phony profiles,
Nine dudes from Jersey,
Eight uptight physicians,
Seven smooth musicians,
Six guys wanting hookups,
Five guys who shave more of their bodies than I do,
Four fun days in Vegas,
Three convicted felons,
Two e-mails from women,
And no man worth my membership fee.

When Push Came to Shove

Even though I had deactivated my membership on one of the more expensive sites two years ago, they sent me matches. Apparently, it was a free trial weekend. In a weak moment, I caved and purchased the cheapest plan. There were many new faces in the sea of familiar faces, most of which were still "outside of my parameters." That means they aren't really matches, but they had to send me someone.

One guy, just outside of my parameters, contacted me. He did not have animals and was funny on the phone. He had a penchant for sports, particularly football. We did not share many interests. However, we shared common viewpoints on things such as politics and religion. Despite not being my usual type, I thought I would give him a chance.

Then, I got bronchitis. I should have recognized that as an omen. But I didn't. We postponed our first date.

Two weeks later, he brought me a gift on our first date—a wine glass filled with chocolate. That was sweet, literally and figuratively.

He seemed reserved. I attempted to get him to open up more. He loved talking about Florida. It was his happy place. Southern Florida was definitely not my happy place. Too hot and humid for me.

He swore he was going to exercise and lose at least sixty pounds. I offered to help him with healthier meal alternatives. However, I could tell, this would be a constant uphill battle. Everything he consumed was breaded and/or fried and drowning in a bottomless lake of cheese.

He loved talking on the phone. He would call at least twice a day, sometimes more often, even when I would be seeing him that day. I told him once I started writing again, I would not be able to talk during the day. It would break my concentration.

I kept trying to convince myself that these were minor things. I had to stop being so picky.

After a couple weeks, he commented that he stopped taking his medication. All of it. Well, that wasn't a good thing. He did not consult his doctor.

He became more aggressive, and his comments were increasingly mean-spirited. He criticized my clothes. Mind you, he wore T-shirts and cargo shorts most of the time. But he made sure to let me know he wanted me to look nice for him. I mentioned it would be nice if he made an effort for me. It fell on mostly deaf ears.

One day, he began shoving me and roughhousing with me. Guys do that to each other, but I am not a guy. And I don't do that. I told him to stop. He laughed it off.

In my foyer, I have a bench for people to sit on while putting on their shoes. He refused to sit on it. Instead, he would put his filthy shoes on the bench to tie them. Even after telling him repeatedly not to do that, he still did it and ignored me.

Then he announced one day that he was going to watch his ex-wife's dog while she was on vacation.

I questioned, "At her house, right?"

"No. I'm bringing the dog to my house."

"Then I can't ever go to your house again."

"It's only for four days. I'll vacuum."

"That won't work."

He insisted it would.

I explained in great detail why that would not work. He did not grasp the concept of anaphylaxis and how the dog's dander and hair in his ductwork and on every surface in his house would trigger that for me.

I then offered three workable options of what the ex-wife could do with her dog. I even offered to pay to put the dog in a kennel to avoid contact. I thought then he would understand the gravity of the situation. Nope.

Before that disaster had the opportunity to play out, I encountered the straw that broke the camel's back. I was bent over, tying my sneakers, when he pushed me. I lost my balance and fell forward. If there hadn't been a wall in front of me, I would have ended up falling to the ground.

He laughed.

Angry, I yelled, "Are you crazy? I could have gotten hurt."

Still laughing, he said, "You're overreacting."

Infuriated, I argued, "No, I'm not. Don't you *ever* push me again."

"You need to lighten up."

That was it. I had had enough.

The blatant disrespect and aggressiveness was too much for me to handle. Honestly, I was afraid it would escalate. There was no way I was going to stick around to find out.

He confronted me, "Your attitude toward me has changed."

Yes, because you've become a crazy person who is physically and verbally abusive.

What followed was a breakup conversation that was long overdue.

The creepy part of this story occurred days later. He just happened to show up at a grocery store at the exact same time I was there shopping. He followed me around that store for a good thirty minutes. He pretended to talk on his cell phone. I deliberately walked to the opposite end of the store to get away from him.

As I compared labels between products, he came right over and stood next to me. He didn't say anything. Neither did I. I wasn't sure if he wanted to talk or if he was attempting to intimidate me. More annoyed than scared, I walked away. That did not deter him. With no other option, I finally just left the store, praying he would not follow me.

I don't know what he did after that. All I know is that my ADT security system and I spent a quiet night together.

Jumping Off The Crazy Train

I am done. After that last guy, I'm done. I mean completely, utterly, positively done with online dating. It has brought me nothing but heartache, headaches, and grief.

Okay, okay, I did get a lot of free meals, attended some great shows, amassed a ton of good writing material, and enjoyed one vacation. However, I am no closer to finding a match than I was on the first day I signed up for these services four years ago.

This entire experience has left me physically, mentally, and emotionally exhausted. Dating should be fun and exciting. But somehow, online dating sucked the joy right out of me. It became less about finding a soulmate and more about settling for someone who didn't drive me absolutely crazy. Alas, that didn't work either.

Despite my best efforts, I am not celebrating the thrill of victory. I am wallowing in the agony of defeat. I have even gained weight to the point where my pants no longer fit. I'm writing this wearing sweatpants with a drawstring waist. There's no elastic, just a drawstring. That's a sure sign of hopelessness, if there ever was one.

The definition of insanity is doing the same thing over and over expecting a different result. I just cancelled every online dating account and jumped off the crazy train.

I am reevaluating everything. Why the hell am I still in Indiana? There is nothing keeping me here.

New York was and will always be home. Although, I don't want to move back to the land of high taxes and lake effect snow. I do miss the food and being a five-minute drive from Lake Ontario. But my parents moved to Fort Myers, Florida. So, home is not home anymore in that respect.

Before you say that I should move to Florida, Florida is not my happy place. It's too freaking hot and humid.

I need a change. A radical change. Something unexpected. Something I should have done years ago.

After some deep soul searching, I have reached the decision to leave Indiana. I have no idea where I am going to go. But I am convinced I have to move. I can sell my house and all of my worldly goods and work for the National Park Service.

Mountains, lakes, and hiking trails are my happy places. Since I can't find a man to be happy with, at least I'll be in a happy place. Well, as long as the happy place does not have big bugs, a lot of bees, mosquitoes carrying God-knows-what-virus, ticks with Lyme disease, snakes, or bears.

Hey, I didn't say it was a perfect plan. I'm still brainstorming!

Expect the Unexpected

As I debated the advantages of Colorado versus Nevada, I accepted an invitation from a fellow author to get together and discuss the local author scene. Authors and poets do this from time to time to reassure ourselves that we don't belong on The Island of Misfit Toys.

I met this author through the Annual Christmas Gift & Hobby Show at the Indiana State Fairgrounds. I have been the coordinator for the local authors' booth for many years. Last year, he sat next to me on the last day of the show. Originally, I did not place him next to me. He was slated for the opposite side of the booth. However, at the last minute, I switched his position.

After a long week, I thought having someone next to me who wrote humorous books would be refreshing. He was a few years older than me and appeared shy. But when he told a story, he became quite animated. He was clever, from the East Coast, and most of all, he made me laugh.

I knew getting together with him would be entertaining, and I needed a distraction. He had tons of stories about his cats, his kids, and his adventurous past.

One month after the show, we had time in our schedules to meet.

We discussed whether to meet for coffee or dinner. The weather report predicted a wicked ice storm.

I decided if I was going to risk life and limb in an ice storm, it would be for dinner. Assuming we would pay for our own meals, I suggested an Italian restaurant. I had a gift card *and* a coupon.

He thought he was being funny when he countered with a corner table at White Castle.

I think not!

Then he surprised me by suggesting an upscale restaurant.

I quickly agreed. They had valet. That minimized the chance of killing myself on a patch of ice.

He had met that last online dating guy at the Christmas show. So, he asked if my boyfriend would have a problem with us meeting for dinner.

When I replied that we had broken up, he celebrated.

I was surprised by his response. This was supposed to be a business meeting. But then I recalled that he had five cats. Yup, count them, five cats. So, I knew this wouldn't be going anywhere, even if he was interested in dating.

He claimed to have made reservations under, "Clooney and McAdams."

That was just the beginning. Next, we had a bizarre discussion about what he would wear. His ideas included bicycle shorts and a kilt. I nixed those and suggested a Harley jacket and assless chaps. Although, part of me was worried he might actually wear them.

My worries were unfounded. He dressed pretty conservatively. It felt as if we were old friends catching up after not seeing one another for a few years. I was fascinated by his stories. He had followed his dream of being a professional musician and succeeded. Now, he was an author, with six published books. I lamented that instead of following my dreams, I worked in the automotive industry for over two decades. Now, I was trying to make up for lost time.

We could have talked all night. Alas, the restaurant closed early due to the ice storm raging outside.

As we waited for the valet, I shivered in my pretty winter coat. Good winter coats are big, puffy, and warm. I really wished I had my ugly winter coat instead of the thin pretty one. As I morphed into a human popsicle, he had no coat and was perfectly comfortable. The man was a human furnace.

Evidently, all that radiating heat made him completely irresistible. Before I realized it, our lips met, and we kissed.

Dear God in heaven! What a magical kiss!

I thought, *That was my last first kiss.*

As we were caught up in this unexpected and thrilling kiss, the valet snapped us back to reality.

Oh my God, kid! Couldn't you have warmed up the cars a little longer?

As I slipped into my car, all I could think of was when I would see him again.

Distracted by that kiss, I prayed a Rosary as I drove home. Half of it was to make sure I didn't end up in a ditch. The other half was that he wanted to see me again.

The icy roads were treacherous. However, I was a woman with a new mission. I had to talk to him again. Oh, who was I kidding? I had to kiss those lips again.

The meddling, logical side of my brain shouted, "But he has five freaking cats! It will never work."

The romantic in me argued, "Love will find a way."

"Nope. You're wrong. And love? Are you nuts? You just met the guy. You've had one date."

"Yes, but, what if, by some miracle, he is the one man for me?"

My rational side yelled, "Hello, Suzanne! He has five cats. Not just one, but five! Five cats to deliver certain death."

A calm washed over me. "But I have a feeling about him."

Logical me disagreed, "You've said this before. And where has it gotten you? Heartbroken. Time and time again. Don't put yourself through the torture. And have you forgotten you've sworn off dating?"

The dreamer in me insisted, "This time it's different. Vastly different. And I swore off *online* dating, not all dating."

"You're fooling yourself, Suzanne. This relationship is doomed. I tell you—doomed! Forget it. Forget him. Don't be stupid. Concentrate on your future and moving out of this state."

"I can't."

"You don't even know if he's really interested. This could all be in your head. It's just a crazy, romantic fantasy. Stop before it's too late!"

"It's already too late. I can not explain it. But this is him. I can feel it. I am done looking. This is the man who will set my soul on fire. I just know it in my heart of hearts. This is the man I will love for the rest of my life."

"How can you possibly know that?"

"Isn't it totally obvious? God loves testing me. And what better way to test me than send me a perfect soulmate whose life is completely and unequivocally enmeshed with five cats?"

Epilogue

I know you are dying to know what happened. Well, since we are both authors, he proposed that we write a, "He Said/She Said," book about our story. I agreed. It was a splendid idea!

Spoiler alert! That humorous book is entitled, "Finally! An Unexpected Love Story." I might be a bit biased, but I think our back-and-forth banter is hysterical.

What's so hysterical about it?

Imagine if you will a woman, from Upstate New York, with twelve years of Catholic school education and rules under her belt, who is deathly allergic to all animals, finding her perfect match in a multiple cat-owning, rule-hating guy, who grew up on a farm in a rural mountain town in Pennsylvania.

Our jointly-written book tackles our unexpected, unusual, and often challenging courtship with humor. There are indeed two sides to every story. However, my side is the right side. Just don't tell him that yet. Eventually, he will figure it out on his own.

We have discussed turning our joint project into a play or a sitcom. An updated twist on, *Green Acres*, or even, *The Odd Couple*, might work. We have enough material that the possibilities are endless.

Don't miss out on the rest of my epic saga. I guarantee it is a love

EPILOGUE

story that will have you believing in destiny and that the power of love conquers all.

About The Author

Suzanne grew up in Webster, NY. She is graduate of Our Lady of Mercy High School, Rochester, NY. She obtained a Bachelor of Science degree from GMI Engineering & Management Institute, Flint, MI. She earned a Master of Science degree from Kettering University, Flint, MI. Suzanne worked for General Motors/Delphi for twenty-two years.

Suzanne began telling stories at a very early age and perfected her writing skills and sarcastic wit in high school and college. Friends and family encouraged her to write a book. She tackled that challenge while recovering from cancer several years ago.

Thus far, she has two romantic suspense novels published, *Embracing Destiny* and *Challenging Destiny*. The novels are a mixture of mystery, romance, and humor that create exciting adventures for the characters and readers alike.

Her poetry book, *From 14 to 41,* contains a soulful blend of love, loss, whimsical, and inspirational pieces.

Her blog, *Pursuing My Passion*, features her humorous observations on life.

Suzanne has lived in Noblesville, IN for the past twenty-four years.

ABOUT THE AUTHOR

Suzanne loves to hear from her readers!

If you enjoyed this book,
please leave a review on Amazon or Goodreads!

Check out the latest news and events on Suzanne's website:
www.suzannepurewal.com

www.ingramcontent.com/pod-product-compliance
Lightning Source LLC
Chambersburg PA
CBHW050123020526
44112CB00035B/2365